MEMOIRS OF A WESTCHESTER REALTOR

HALF A CENTURY OF PROPERTY DEVELOPMENT

in Westchester County and Southwestern Connecticut

Memoirs

OF A

Westchester

Realtor

By GEORGE HOWE

ILLUSTRATED

EXPOSITION PRESS   NEW YORK

Exposition Press Inc., 386 Park Avenue, So., New York 16, N.Y.

FIRST EDITION

CONTENTS

INTRODUCTION

IN WRITING THESE REMINISCENCES, 1 have been guided by a desire to place on record many events that have contributed to the development of the most attractive suburban area just north of New York City including Westchester County and nearby Connecticut. I certainly can give first hand testimony as to the desirability and soundness of real estate as an investment. Well-chosen real estate for residential or business use has come through all the ups and downs of booms and depressions with flying colors. A family with its own home in a good environment certainly enjoys an atmosphere of happiness and success.

The tremendous development of New York City which is now the main center of this world's activities, has created such a congestion that many families have moved to the suburbs. Also, many families who have moved to New York for business or other reasons have sought attractive suburban districts to reside in. The hills of Westchester County, bordered on the west by the famous Hudson River and on the east by Greenwich, Connecticut, and the beautiful waters of Long Island Sound have always appealed very strongly to families searching for an ideal homeplace.

In my fifty years of experience in the real estate brokerage field, I have witnessed a very rapid evolution in the development of Westchester County and the adjoining areas of nearby Connecticut, resulting in the building of small cities, villages and beautiful residential parks which make it one of the most attractive suburban areas in this country. Those who live there love it, those who have had any part in its development are very proud of it. It is therefore easy to understand my enthusiasm whenever I discuss Westchester County or nearby Connecticut.

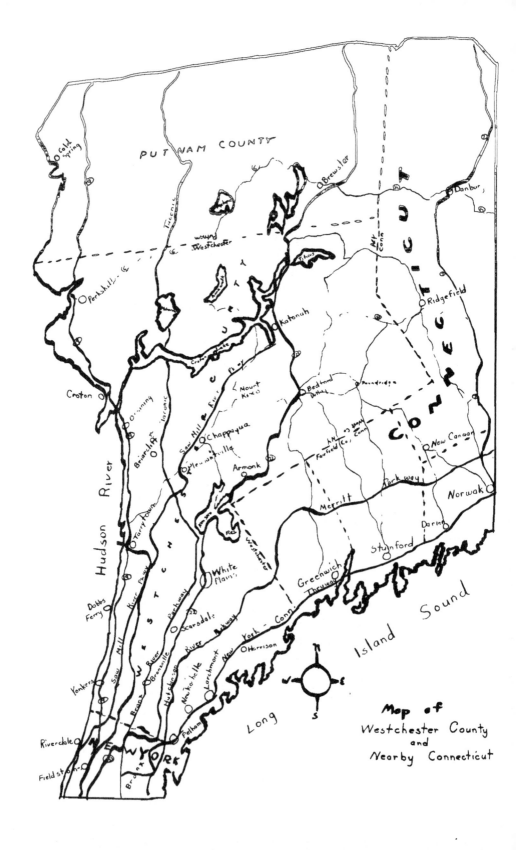

Map of
Westchester County
and
Nearby Connecticut

CHAPTER I

A BRIEF OUTLINE OF WESTCHESTER COUNTY AND NEARBY CONNECTICUT

As a REAL-ESTATE BROKER specializing in the sale of suburban and country properties in Westchester County and nearby Connecticut, it has been my pleasure and privilege to see at firsthand the wonderful development of this beautiful suburban area north of New York City. As I ride around and see the splendid boulevards and highways, the charming residential districts, the very active cities and villages with their numerous new public buildings, schools, parks, and their commercial and industrial districts, I can hardly believe my eyes.

I must say that I have had the pleasure of meeting and knowing intimately many prominent and admirable citizens, and my happy experiences in dealing with them have made me a confirmed optimist.

In reciting these pleasant reminiscences, I have made no effort to describe in great detail the transactions in which I have taken part. Some errors and omissions, including the incorrect spelling of some names, and other inaccuracies may appear, but I have tried to avoid them. The many real estate transactions, as well as the buyers and sellers in this brief story are very interesting.

Fifty years ago Westchester and the northern suburbs were real country districts. Even Washington Heights in New York City and the Upper Bronx seemed far away, and included many suburban estates and open fields. Beyond this was beautiful Spuyten Duyvil and Riverdale, with their luxurious estates along the Hudson. Nearby was the very large and historic Van Cortlandt Park. North of this was the City of Yonkers, east of which was the City of Mount Vernon, and east of this the Village of Pelham on Long Island Sound.

To reach these districts there were a few main highways and trolley lines. Also there were the elevated railroads in New York City along Second, Third, Sixth and Ninth Avenues running to the upper areas of the city. But the main means of travel to and from the city to its northern suburbs were the New York Central Railroad, running along the Hudson River, the Putnam Division of the New York Central Railroad with its two branches, one running to the City Hall in Yonkers and the other running through central Westchester County toward Lake Mahopac terminating at Carmel in lower Dutchess County.

Also, there was the Harlem Division of the New York Central Railroad running north through White Plains to Brewster and beyond, thus providing easy access to the easterly areas of Westchester and Putnam counties. Finally, there was the New York, New Haven and Hartford Railroad running northeasterly along Long Island Sound through Mount Vernon, Pelham, New Rochelle, Rye, Greenwich, Stamford, and nearby Connecticut.

With very few automobiles and few main highways, practically all New York business men who lived in the northern suburbs were railroad commuters. As the commuting trains were drawn by coal-burning locomotives with their resulting dirt, noise, and smoke, commuting was no joy. All the railroad lines running through Westchester terminated in New York City at the Grand Central Station, except the Putnam Division of the New York Central which terminated at 155th Street in Manhattan at the end of the Ninth Avenue elevated railroad. Commuting on this line was convenient for business men with offices in the downtown Wall Street areas because they could take the Ninth Avenue elevated express trains which ran from the Wall Street area to 155th Street, Manhattan, then they could get out and walk a short distance ahead on the same platform to a Putnam Division train, get aboard and go home to the Upper Bronx, to the Van Cortlandt Park area beyond and then into South Yonkers on the Putnam branch which terminated at Getty Square in the center of Yonkers. Another branch of the Putnam ran into Central and northern Westchester.

Trains on the Putnam Division of the New York Central Railroad made stops at the Main Line station of the New York Central at High Bridge in the Bronx where one could switch to the main line trains and go south to Grand Central Station or north along the Hudson River. The South Yonkers branch of the Putnam Division had stations at Lowerre, Park Hill and Getty Square.

Easy and quick commuting helped greatly in developing the residential area of Park Hill in South Yonkers, which I will discuss later.

I was born in and grew up in a suburban area on the banks of the Mississippi River in New Orleans, Louisiana. When I graduated as an electrical engineer from Tulane University I decided to come to New York to live, as it stood out in my dreams as the greatest city in the world. When I arrived in New York my first position was with the New York Edison Company where, among other duties, I was assigned to make tests of the use of electricity in New York City in business and industry. I soon saw at firsthand the great speed with which the city was growing.

I made many inspection trips to the suburban areas. I well remember my first visit to the Washington Heights district overlooking the Hudson River in Upper Manhattan. This high, beautiful hilltop area with fine country homes and parklike surroundings seemed quite remote from the business areas of New York. North of Washington Heights was the upper end of Manhattan. Beyond this was the famous Spuyten Duyvil Creek connecting the Harlem River with the Hudson River, thus making Manhattan an island. Beyond Spuyten Duyvil Creek was a magnificent ridge of high land overlooking the Hudson River, known as Spuyten Duyvil and Riverdale-on-the-Hudson, where many luxurious estates had been built. North of this along the Hudson one came to Yonkers, a teeming city which had already been extensively developed, especially the business and industrial areas where large plants of the Otis Elevator Company and the Alexander Smith Carpet factory were located. The residential sections of Yonkers included Park Hill in South Yonkers and North Broadway in North Yonkers.

North of Yonkers along the Hudson were the charming but thinly developed villages of Hastings, Dobbs Ferry, Irvington, Tarrytown, Ossining and Croton.

Along the Harlem Division of the New York Central Railroad in central and eastern Westchester, much progress and activity was under way. Mount Vernon, an active city north of New York, was making rapid strides. Beyond this, Lawrence Park, Bronxville, was rapidly developing, guided by the energy and the imaginative genius of Mr. W. Lawrence. It was indeed becoming a very choice residential area, with the attractive Gramatan Hotel at its center. Beyond this, Scarsdale, Hartsdale and White Plains were growing. Along the shores of Long Island Sound, Pelham Manor had been beautifully built up. Beyond this, the teeming young city of New Rochelle was alive with progress. Then came Larchmont, Mamaroneck, Rye, Greenwich and Connecticut. The lovely shore-front districts and excellently planned business and residential areas presented a most tempting picture for real-estate development.

CHAPTER II

I BEGAN MY REAL-ESTATE CAREER

I COULD EASILY SEE the opportunity that this wonderful suburban area offered to energetic workers in the real-estate business. It lured me so strongly that I decided to enter this field. I made my first real estate connection with the American Real Estate Company, a very large and successful company which, among its many activities, was developing a most attractive and desirable suburban residential park known as Park Hill-on-the-Hudson, situated on a magnificent hill-top location overlooking Yonkers and the Hudson River. Down in front of it was the Park Hill station of the Putnam Division of the New York Central Railroad. The main office of the American Real Estate Company was located at 527 Fifth Avenue, corner of 44th Street, in New York, and I was attracted by the excellent advertisements which it had put in the New York Sunday papers inviting home seekers to inspect and consider living in Park Hill. After inspection, I was thoroughly sold on the property myself, and after several interviews decided to enter the real-estate field with the American Real Estate Company. They gave me a desk at the main office and told me to use the branch office at Park Hill as occasion required, and especially to be there to meet customers on Saturdays, Sundays and other holidays when people would likely come in answer to the newspaper advertisements. I was given copies of the booklets describing the property, along with names of people who had inquired about it. They permitted me, if necessary, to engage an automobile in New York at their expense and take a prospective customer from the city on a tour of inspection to Park Hill, on the way passing through beautiful Van Cortlandt Park. It can be readily seen why, with this help and the very attractive and desirable building sites and excellent houses for sale, I made sales.

Before going further, let me describe Park Hill-on-the-Hudson and its charms. As previously stated, it was situated in South Yonkers at the Park Hill Station of the Putnam Division of the New York Central Railroad. On the west side of the station there was an attractive park extending to South Broadway, Yonkers. There was an excellent driveway through this park from South Broadway to the parking area at the railroad station. On the south side of this park was the large and beautifully planned Park Hill Inn. Its spacious dining rooms, terraces and fine service attracted a host of enthusiastic followers who came there frequently from New York after a pleasant automobile drive, or to entertain guests. I remember meeting many important people there, including Harry Sinclair, a frequent visitor who developed the Sinclair Oil Company. Many other leaders in industry and finance found it a delightful place to enjoy the best of good food.

On the east side of the Park Hill Station was a hill of considerable height, at the top of which was a large and beautiful rolling plateau with many attractive streets and avenues on which there were many exceptionally charming home sites commanding magnificent views. On these sites lovely houses had been built or were being built for exacting buyers.

lower elevator house and real estate office, Park Hill-on-Hudson.

Upper elevator house, Park Hill.

The railroad station was at the foot of Park Hill. Opposite the railroad station there was the American Real Estate Company's real-estate office and a waiting room at the lower end of an inclined elevator which took passengers from the foot of the hill to the top, ending in an upper-elevator house, which included a waiting room with a large open sight-seeing porch from which there were magnifi-

Estate of Mr. E. K. Martin, Park Hill.   View of South Yonkers, Hudson River and Palisades from Park Hill.

cent views of the Hudson River and the Palisades. Down below in the foreground one saw the other residential areas of South Yonkers covering about one-half mile between Park Hill and the Hudson River. West of Park Hill, on the river front, was the Ludlow station on the main line of the New York Central Railroad. This was an excellent advantage, because if a commuter from Park Hill wished to use the main line of the New York Central for some reason he could easily go to the Ludlow station. The inclined elevator leading to the top of the hill was available without charge to all residents of Park Hill and their visitors. Those building sites on the front hilltop avenues of Park Hill enjoying magnificent views were in great demand. A fine roadway had been built from the Park Hill railroad station to the hilltop area, making the whole hilltop district accessible by foot, carriage or automobile.

When a customer landed at the Park Hill Station and came to the real-estate office for information, one of the brokers took him in hand. There were usually several of us on the job. Mr. Guy Short, a very devoted and reliable secretary, had charge of the office with permanent headquarters there, so that if any of the brokers' clients came along when the broker himself was not there, Guy Short took over the job of showing the client around. When a customer appeared at the office and was assigned to me, I proceeded, after a brief inquiry into his requirements, to take him up the hill on the inclined elevator. When we reached the upper-elevator house I took him on the scenic front porch and showed him the magnificent scenery. He and his wife, or others in his party, usually became so entranced that I had to pull them away. On the road in front of the upper-elevator house there awaited an open surrey drawn by a handsome horse which the company provided for inspection trips throughout the property. I would put my customers in the carriage, take the reins and proceed to drive around the streets, showing the many building sites and houses for sale, pointing out the Park Hill Country Club which had been built for Park Hill residents, with its fine tennis courts and other attractions. I would show the customer the lovely homes for sale and call his attention to the exceptional advantages that Park Hill offered, which made it the ideal location for a permanent homeplace.

If after finding a suitable house, the client needed assistance in financing the purchase, the company helped him if he was a good risk. If he could not find any suitable house, I showed him various building sites which I thought might appeal to him and his family. The company employed an architect and building superintendent who were on hand in a construction office on the property. I would take the client to this office, explain his requirements to the architect who, with the co-operation of the construction superintendent, would give a rough estimate of the cost of the proposed house. Finally, when a rough outline had been agreed upon, the architect, within a few days, provided a drawing of the proposed house on the chosen site, including plans of its layout. If these proved satisfactory, detailed building plans and specifications and a final estimate of the cost were submitted. If the customer was satisfied, as he usually was, the company would prepare a contract through its law office agreeing to build the house and, if the customer desired, arranged the financing of its purchase from the company on satisfactory terms.

At the time when all this occurred, there were very few real-estate development companies which provided such services so reasonably and delivered the final product with such quality and efficiency. Park Hill naturally attracted many buyers. I remember the first sale that I made was to Mr. George DuBois, a prominent New York business-man. When he mentioned his name, I was reminded of some friends of that name in New Orleans, Louisiana. He said that he was related to them, and we had a very pleasant inspection tour together, winding up with my first real-estate sale of a very nice house. Needless to say I was thrilled and very happy.

As days and months and years rolled by, the office at Park Hill

The DuBois residence in Park Hill, Yonkers, my first sale.   The Fields property on King Street, Chappaqua.

made many sales. I rented a room and opened my own real-estate office with my own secretary in the same building as the American Real Estate Company in New York, and planned to extend my activities. Park Hill rapidly grew in size and population. Many families chose it as their place of residence, among them were Adolph Pincoffs, eminent New York lawyer, James B. Lackey, a leader in the street-car advertising field, George H. Doran, and Casper W. Hodson, both well-known publishers, Dennis F. O'Brien, counsel for Douglas Fairbanks and Mary Pickford; also, there were Richard Bennett, the actor, Dr. Cyrus Townsend Brady, author and preacher, Irvin S. Cobb, humorist, C. E. Sheppard, printer and publisher, Robert Boettger, manufacturer, Owen Davis, playwright, Dr. C. S. Green, osteopath, each highly esteemed in his field, and many, many others.

I remember the attractive balls at the Park Hill Country Club and the very interesting tennis matches held there. The social life of the community was ideal. Many residents would get together and take strolls on Sunday afternoons and sometimes stop in at the Park Hill real-estate office for a visit. I remember the delightful visits of a group that often strolled together, including the famous newspaper columnist Franklin P. Adams, Richard T. Lingley, an executive of the American Real Estate Company with whom he visited, Irvin Cobb, and George Doran. Irvin Cobb would tell his humorous stories of Negro life in the South, using the words, gestures and pronunciation of the Negro.

He was a wonderful actor and usually had everyone in listening distance roaring with laughter. Even when he retold a joke, it seemed to be fresh and just as funny and entertaining as a new one.

In every way Park Hill was indeed a most desirable homeplace. I moved there myself with my family, and we greatly enjoyed its many advantages. The American Real Estate Company had a fine group of executive officers, some of whom had moved to Park Hill, including E. K. Martin, one of its founders and president, who had a beautiful home on Alta Avenue overlooking the Hudson River. Mr. Francis Sisson, another officer, built a lovely home on a sightly location. Richard T. Lingley, one of the principal executives and Austin L. Babcock, another executive officer, built their homes there.

The company had grown up under a plan of financing which included the sales of American Real Estate Company debenture bonds which were offered for investment paying 6 per cent interest and permitting redemption for cash if the holder desired. In addition to Park Hill, the company had been very successful in developing real estate in Manhattan and the Bronx including apartment houses and office buildings. Its bonds were highly regarded and were sold extensively in the New York and New England areas. Even though the company prospered, its one weakness was the prepayment privilege of its bonds, so when occasions arose due to our then poor and inadequate banking system when banks even though sound could not get cash from the government to pay depositors, the holders of American Real Estate Company bonds could present their bonds for redemption in cash.

Such an incident occurred in 1916. A holder of American Real Estate Company bonds came to New York from New England to get money from that company by cashing in his bonds when his local bank could not help him. He presented his bonds at the New York office for redemption. He received payment in cash, and was so delighted that when he returned home, he spread the news widely among his friends, and the story was published in newspapers telling how A.R.E. Co. bonds were the soundest of investments and could be cashed promptly by anyone needing cash. Immediately a flood of redemption requests showered upon the New York office. When cash on hand ran out, the company itself being unable to get cash from the banks, it had to refuse redemption requests and was forced into receivership. This ended the career of an otherwise very successful real-estate corporation.

CHAPTER III

THE RAPID GROWTH OF THE NORTHERLY SUBURBS

DURING THE PERIOD of my activity at Park Hill, great improvement in transportation was taking place. The automobile was coming into general use in traveling to and from the suburbs. This encouraged the building and paving of many roads. Also, the New York Subway system was rapidly being developed. The Broadway branch of the subway had been extended to Van Cortlandt Park at Broadway and 242nd Street, Manhattan, in 1908. From the end of the subway a passenger could take a trolley car which ran along Broadway on the side of Van Cortlandt Park in New York connecting with South Broadway in Yonkers and ride to Park Hill and other neighboring areas. The improvement in transportation greatly stirred the development all along the upper west side of New York, including Washington Heights, Riverdale and South Yonkers. The Delafield estate proceeded to develop a large tract of its property in Riverdale as a suburban park of the very first quality which it named "Fieldston." The famous Horace Mann School for Boys of New York moved uptown into this area.

A section of South Yonkers along Valentine Lane just beyond the New York City line called Van Cortlandt Terrace was developed. Also on Valentine Lane, the American Real Estate Company acquired a tract of land which it named the Lawrence Property and proceeded to develop. I was asked to take charge of this development along with my other duties on Park Hill, and proceeded to do so actively. Shortly afterwards, I, with several associates, organized a company which we called Valentine Terrace, Inc., to develop a tract of land at the corner of Valentine Lane and Riverdale Avenue in South Yonkers which we purchased from Mr. Ludlow. A few years before all of this area had been for private homes, now it began to attract apartment houses, and much of the land in Valentine Terrace was sold for this purpose.

I might add that simultaneously the building of apartment houses increased rapidly in Washington Heights and in the lower end of Riverdale and Spuyten Duyvil. New York City was certainly pushing up rapidly into this suburban area. This was the period before World

War I and while this expansion of housing in the Riverdale and South Yonkers areas was taking place, extensive real estate development occurred in Mount Vernon, Pelham, New Rochelle, Larchmont and Rye along Long Island Sound and also throughout Central Westchester extending northward through Bronxville, Scarsdale, White Plains and beyond.

We Opened Our Office in Pelham

This expansion impressed me so strongly that I expanded my office and its activities. When the American Real Estate Company folded up in 1916, I opened a branch office in Pelham at the corner of Pelhamdale Avenue and the Boston Post Road, and began to list properties for sale in that region. I employed William J. Eshback as manager of the Pelham office, and he, with excellent skill and ability, soon placed it among the leaders in this area.

World War I threw a cold blanket on real-estate activity and slowed its growth, but did not stop it. In fact, even with the financial crisis and other economic troubles which followed the war, my office continued to be busy.

Shortly after opening my Pelham office in 1916, we were asked by the owners of Larchmont Gardens in Larchmont to take charge of the sale of its property. This was indeed a most interesting and attractive residential development situated within walking distance of the New Haven railroad station in Larchmont. Through this property ran a very active brook, which came to a point where a sudden drop in its bed made an attractive waterfall. From there it ran into a lower area which had been dammed up, creating a lovely lake. Overlooking the waterfall and the lake, a combination real-estate office and club house had been built. Through an imposing archway at the entrance to the property, a boulevard led to the lake and the club house. From this center, extending in all directions, were exceptionally well-planned streets and roadways that presented an inviting picture to the home seeker. I appointed as manager of the Larchmont office a most attractive, energetic and capable lady, Mrs. Ida M. Parent, who had previously been active in real estate in this district. With great skill and energy, she put new life into Larchmont Gardens and made it grow with increasing speed.

We Extended Our Activities

While this was going on, my offices became active in many other districts. We made our first sale in Greenwich, Connecticut, by selling in May, 1916, in co-operation with a local broker, the estate of Mrs. Mary W. Jones in Belle Haven, Greenwich, to Mr. Theodore Sengstak. In connection with this sale there was another first which

Former Sengstak house in Belle Haven, Greenwich.

Former Yandel Estate sold to Ernest G. Brown on Rock Craig Road, Greenwich.

we often mention. There was a young lawyer in Greenwich named William S. Hirschberg who had become the junior member of a law firm named Wright and Hirschberg. At the closing of the title to the property of Mrs. Jones which took place in my office at 527 Fifth Avenue, New York, Mr. Hirschberg came representing Mrs. Jones. His firm is now the well-known Greenwich law firm of Hirschberg, Pettengill and Strong, and Mr. Hirschberg tells me that the Jones closing of title in my office in New York was the first that he attended in his long and magnificent career. Incidentally, Mrs. Jones was the sister of the political leader and industrialist, the late Mr. William L. Ward, a partner in the metal-manufacturing firm of Russell, Burdsall and Ward, of Portchester. He was, in my judgment, one of the great men of his time.

Central Park Avenue, which ran northward into Central Westchester passing through Van Cortlandt Park and ending at White Plains, was beginning to come into prominence. It is now one of the main arteries of travel. Our activities increased at this time northward into Upper Westchester County, and in October, 1916, we sold the Gardiner estate in Ossining in co-operation with Mr. Travis to Mr. H. A. Gordon, and in March, 1917, we sold in co-operation with Edward V. Siedle (now one of the leading Westchester brokers with an office in Rye) the Locust Ridge Farm on the Whippoorwill Road, Chappaqua, to Dr. W. H. Sheldon. The following month we sold the Porter estate in Cold Spring, on the Hudson, in co-operation with Robert T. Wood, former counsel of the American Real Estate Company, and William J. Yates, a young man who lived in Cold Spring and became one of the most active brokers in our office. He later developed his own very highly considered real-estate office in Ossining.

Our activities continued to increase rapidly and, a few months later, I sold for investment the Wilbur Whitson farm estate on the Pines Bridge Road in Ossining and other properties nearby in Chappaqua to W. H. McDonough, a New York business executive. These and other sales in northern Westchester, in addition to our activities in Yonkers, Riverdale, Pelham and Larchmont indicate how our office grew up preparing itself to handle properties for sale throughout Westchester County and Connecticut. As a result, I can report that I have seen at firsthand, and often taken personally a very active part in, the extensive development of this area. This fact has prompted me to write these accounts of some of the sales in which I took part, the memory of which has always been a source of great pleasure.

CHAPTER IV

THE HUDSON RIVER DISTRICT

IN THOSE DAYS, the dream of a wealthy family coming to New York to live was to own a handsome estate overlooking the Hudson River within reasonable commuting distance of the city. To them this was paradise. In nearby Spuyten Duyvil and Riverdale, were located the fine estates of the illustrious Johnson family, Lee de Forrest, inventor of the radio tube, Archibald Douglas, E. C. Delafield, banker, Cleveland Dodge, capitalist, George W. Perkins, a partner of J. P. Morgan and Company, and many other notable families. In Yonkers there were the estates of great leaders including Alexander Smith Cochran, James B. Colgate, J. B. Trevor, J. E. Andrus, B. E. Kingman, A. R. Bailey, C. S. Chittenden, Anna C. Ewing, Samuel Untermeyer, Mrs. Thomas Ewing, Gertrude Thompson, C. C. Dula and Mrs. H. S. Duell. In Hastings and Dobbs Ferry there were, among others, the estates of E. C. Moore, Daniel Draper, Albert Shaw, Oswald Villard, Morton Paton, J. B. Russell, Walston H. Brown and Edwin Gould. In Ardsley and Irvington, in addition to the beautiful estates in Ardsley Park, there were the estates of Philip Schuyler, C. D. Fraser, Carol Victor, A. L. Barber, Allen Townsend, M. S. Beltzhoover, Hugh Hill, Daniel G. Reid, Adam K. Luke, Caroline Rutter, J. B. Whitehouse, C. H. Matthiessen, F. E. Randall, Virginia Stern, Mary E. Eddison, T. C. Millett, the Sayles Estate and the historic estate of Washington Irving.

Beyond Irvington, in Tarrytown, among other estates were those of Russell Hopkins, Isaac N. Seligman, Henry Graves, Jr., John Daniel, William R. Harris, Sidney C. Borg, Mr. Robert B. Dula, Roswell Skeel, Mrs. Finley Sheppard, Reverend Alfred Duane Pell, Lucy Eastman, David L. Luke, Gella Berolzheimer, General Howard Carroll, J. F. Detmer, Jacob Ruppert, Jr., John D. Archbold, R. C. Clowry, John D. Rockefeller, William Rockefeller, Frank A. Vanderlip, and William H. Douglas. This long list of important estates continued northward beyond Poughkeepsie.

As an ambitious real-estate office, we naturally took great interest in this Hudson River District. Therefore, in the spring of 1919, I was very happy to accept the offer made us by the Delafield Estate to take charge of the selling of their property in the beautiful residential park known as Fieldston which they had developed on part of their property in Riverdale, on the Hudson. This was indeed a residential park of the very finest type. We took charge of the real estate office there which became very active, and appointed Edgar G. Johnson as manager. We promptly sold many beautiful building sites to home seekers who built outstanding suburban homes. Among these buyers were Mrs. Fannie S. Rockwood, Dr. L. D. Buckley, Mrs. Elizabeth Banfield, Walter E. Kelly, Philip L. Schell, F. S. Rollins, Robert Bowler, W. P. Hoffman, and many others. We soon found that there was a good market for houses and estates that came on the market for sale in the adjoining Riverdale and Spuyten Duyvil districts. We were specially honored in making the sale to Charles Evans Hughes, Jr., the son of Chief Justice Hughes of the United States Supreme Court, of the Fieldston residence of J. E. Bush, and in selling a residence owned by Mrs. George W. Perkins, wife of the famous banker George W. Perkins, situated near their own home, to Mr. Spruille Braden, one of our leaders in the copper-mining industry, who later became our ambassador to Argentina. We also sold the beatutiful estate of Mr. John Ross Delafield to the New York lawyer Martin Conboy, and later we sold the estate of Mrs. Susan M. Allien to the Passionist Fathers. This institution was situated in New Jersey in inadequate quarters and, considering the high and unselfish ideals of its personnel, it needed a site of some size in an inspiring location. This proved to be the answer. We later sold the residence of Edna H. Musa to James Wallen.

Of all my experiences in the real-estate field, I look back at our activities in Fieldston as being among the most interesting and satisfying. I had occasion to meet and become closely acquainted with many of the great men of that period. I also remember the personal part which I took in selling the Randolph estate, situated on the upper end of Palisade Avenue, to the College of Mount St. Vincent which adjoined the property. The nuns were particularly happy in acquiring the property, and the owners, who were fond of the nuns, were happy that I brought about the sale which kept both sides the best of friends.

During my many years of activity I became very well acquainted with the Johnson Brothers who at one time operated the very successful Johnson Iron Works in the valley along the railroad tracks on Spuyten Duyvil Creek. They had purchased most of the high plateau

Hoffman Estate in Fieldston.

ATTRACTIVE COUNTRY RESIDENCE
ARDSLEY-ON-THE-HUDSON

WITH PRIVATE CHAPEL

The Frank Gould Estate in Ardsley-on-Hudson.

at Spuyten Duyvil surrounding the Monument of Henry Hudson and built their own homes there. It was indeed a location with magnificent views and delightful privacy. It was decided to build a bridge over Spuyten Duyvil Creek and extend the Parkway along Riverside Drive on the Hudson River to connect with the Saw Mill River and Taconic Parkways which were to provide modern automobile routes from New York parallel to the Hudson River. This plan called for a new bridge and parkway to run right through the Johnson properties, changing completely their character as private estates. I realized how much of a shock this must have been to the family and how difficult it would be to reimburse them for the property taken by the parkway. I was employed by them as a real-estate expert to testify for them in the condemnation proceedings, and did my best to obtain an adequate compensation from the court. After much debate and finally by compromise, an award was made, but the parkway ran right along side of the beautiful home of Mr. John Johnson on which he had spent much time and money, and I knew that the family could never be adequately repaid. Photos of the bridge and surroundings are shown on page 28.

Residence in Riverdale sold to the Passionist Fathers.

Fieldston sales office.

The bridge across Spuyten Duyvil extending
the West Side Parkway into Westchester
County, in process of construction.

View of the Hudson River and Palisades from
the Johnson Estate.

CHAPTER V

THE BIRTH OF THE WESTCHESTER REALTY BOARD

IN THE YEAR 1916, real estate brokers doing business in Westchester County finally decided that the rapid development of the many districts in the county made it necessary to establish a schedule of rates of commission, as well as other rules and regulations which all brokers in the county would agree to and thus avoid unnecessary conflicts. A number of the leading members of the profession got together and organized the Westchester County Realty Board, and elected as its first president Charles Field Griffin, a successful broker who was held in the highest esteem by all who knew him. His home was in Mamaroneck, and he specialized in the better properties, including estates along Long Island Sound from New York to Bridgeport, Connecticut. He was one of those who realized fully the need of a real-estate board to establish a uniform code of commissions and ethics to cover all the suburban area of Westchester County.

After the board was organized with headquarters in White Plains, it developed that other areas like Yonkers had established local boards which were independent and did not recognize the rules and regulations of the Westchester Board. It became hard to attract the brokers of Yonkers to join the Westchester Realty Board when there was a local Yonkers Realty Board with headquarters in Yonkers which could keep in closer touch with local conditions and requirements. Thus the competition went on and it soon became evident that the Westchester Realty Board would have to absorb the local boards or establish branch offices in the various communities.

This problem had come up from time to time in other regions in the past and presented many difficulties. For instance, in New York City there is the Real Estate Board of New York, the Brooklyn Realty Board and the Bronx Realty Board, all separate and independent organizations.

With my many years' experience in Yonkers and my growing activities in other sections of Westchester County, I felt the need of establishing uniform rules for the whole county covering the main issues of commissions and ethics, and having branch offices in the various communities to cover local details and conditions. Just how

to do this was a problem. I had been elected president of the Board
in 1921, and I remembered that when I was in college and was a
member of the D.K.E. fraternity it had general offices in New York
and branch chapters in various colleges, all working together in
excellent harmony and unison. It occurred to me that the Westchester
Realty Board should establish chapters in various districts of Westchester County. I discussed the matter with various members of our
board including Stephen L. Angell, a broker in the Scarsdale, White
Plains and Greenburgh areas. Mr. Angell became a very active
advocate of the plan and the board, after some discussion, decided
to adopt the plan. Groups of members of the Westchester Realty
Board in the various centers of Westchester County were organized
and were given charters to operate as chapters of the main board.
I remember the great interest and enthusiasm of the speakers of the
various chapters when, as president of the Westchester County Realty
Board, I presented them, on behalf of the board, with their charters
at a ceremonial dinner at the Gramatan Hotel in Bronxville. Since
then, additional chapters have been organized as various districts
developed, and the Westchester County Realty Board is today one of
the strongest organizations of its kind in the country.

Randolph property sold to the Mount St.   A street scene in Fieldston, Riverdale.
Vincent Convent in Riverdale.

CHAPTER VI

THE GROWTH OF LARCHMONT AND VICINITY

AFTER WORLD WAR I, our office in Larchmont was very active. Also, we were listing properties and making sales in Pelham, New Rochelle, Larchmont and Mamaroneck. The whole Long Island Sound district was developing rapidly.

Our office in Pelham was also very active. Many of our clients bought attractive plots of ground on which they built excellent country homes. Speculative builders became very active, and built many homes which they offered for sale.

The New York, Westchester and Boston Railroad, which was a new line controlled by the New Haven Railroad, opened a branch extending from New York to White Plains running parallel with Weaver Street back of Larchmont and a new line parallel with the New Haven line as far as Port Chester with a special station at Larchmont Gardens. This naturally stimulated real-estate activity in this district. Large estate properties along the shore and hills back of Larchmont grew more popular. One of the important sales which we made was that of the estate of Miles Tierney on Old Mamaroneck Road back of Larchmont to Mr. F. Ducoudray.

The increase in the number of families moving into the Larchmont area brought about a need for country and beach clubs which were then few in number in this district, so we decided to do our best to solve this problem.

Mr. E. Lyman Bill, a very successful publisher, had acquired a large tract of land, situated on the east side of Weaver Street south of Griffin Avenue on the outskirts of Larchmont, which was gently rolling in character with some open fields and beautiful woodland. It commanded long-distance views of the surrounding countryside. He decided to build a palatial residence for his own use on the property, and the house was well advanced in construction when, unfortunately, Mr. Bill died. It was indeed a great shock to his family and friends. The family, after some consideration, decided to sell the property with the house partly built if a suitable purchaser could be found. The property was submitted to us for sale, and I gave the problem a great deal of personal attention. I realized that because of the size of the

Real estate office at Larchmont Gardens.   The club house of the Bonnie Briar Golf Club.

property and the large amount of money required to purchase it, it would be difficult to find a satisfactory buyer. While we were giving great thought to this question, my Larchmont associates, in discussing the problem with neighboring estate owners, including Mr. C. W. Moody who later became a developer, agreed with me that inasmuch as a golf club was needed in the district, the organization of such a club should not be very difficult. I discussed the matter with the executors of the Bill Estate, and they became deeply interested in the plan which we suggested. We succeeded in organizing the Bonnie Briar Country Club and appointed Mr. E. Pierre Willis, a popular local resident, to obtain members among the prominent local families. He indeed made a great success of this effort and later became known as a most able club organizer. We appointed Devereux Emmett, the golf architect, to design a course and proceeded to finish the house as a most interesting and attractive country club. When the club was finally opened, it was indeed an event of note. The Bill family had taken a great deal of interest in the club and assisted greatly its financing, and in the years which followed, it became widely known and admired as one of the finest golf clubs in Westchester County. It still enjoys that reputation today.

As my office grew and extended its activities throughout Westchester County and Connecticut, we opened new offices in many areas.

At one time we had separate offices in Fieldston, Yonkers, Hastings, Bronxville, Pelham, Larchmont, Rye, Greenwich, Stamford and White Plains. Our staff of brokers and office associates was a very interesting and delightful group, and on several occasions we had formal dinner parties in various New York hotels, where the group could get together and celebrate. The picture of one of these parties which we held at the Waldorf Astoria Hotel in New York on December 1, 1920, is shown herein, and it certainly pictures a happy family.

Annual Dinner Party.

That section of Larchmont which lies between the Boston Post Road and Long Island Sound is called Larchmont Manor. It is very beautifully laid out, and is generally considered as being one of the most attractive and desirable suburban districts. Many substantial families had chosen it as their home place and built fine homes and estates. The Larchmont Yacht Club is located on the easterly side of Larchmont Manor, and is highly rated in yachting circles. Down along the shore, in the center of Larchmont Manor, the town had developed a public park with a large bathing beach and bathing facilities. This did not serve all the requirements of the many residents who desired a shore club not only for swimming and beach activities, but also for entertainment and club activities. A suitable site was not available, as all the waterfront locations had been developed with homes and estates. Just at the right time, the magnificent Schaeffer estate in Larchmont Manor came on the market for sale, and we sold it to a group who remodeled it and converted it into the lovely Larchmont Shore Club, which is one of the outstanding shore clubs on the Sound.

On the westerly side of Larchmont Manor, extending from the Boston Post Road to the Sound, was the Premium River, which separated Larchmont from New Rochelle. Running parallel with the Premium River on its easterly side was Pryer Lane in Larchmont along which many beautiful homes had been built. On the westerly side of the Premium River was a large undeveloped tract of land and beyond this was the luxurious suburban park called Premium Point Park in New Rochelle which was approached by its own private entrance from the Boston Post Road. On the Larchmont side of Premium River there was a short road leading from Pryer Lane down to a small wooden bridge across the Premium River which gave access to the undeveloped acreage. In front of this acreage there was an extensive shore front bordering a large waterfront pond known as Premium Mill Pond. This had been dammed up in front of Premium Point Park to retain a high-tide level of water at all tides.

This attractive undeveloped acreage was therefore ideal for the building of beautiful homes like those on both its sides, namely, Premium Point Park in New Rochelle and Larchmont Manor in Larchmont. My associates in our Larchmont Gardens office and several others joined with me in organizing a company to purchase the property from the Pryer family who had owned it for many years. We named the new area Pryer Manor. We built a larger bridge to approach it from Pryer Lane in Larchmont, and planned a residential area with excellent roads, including an outlet on the rear to a road leading to the Boston Post Road in New Rochelle. Needless to say, the property received much favorable comment, and we were successful in promptly making sales of some of the best sites to suitable buyers, one of whom was Anton L. Trunk, a very well-known and successful New York real estate broker who purchased a beautiful site overlooking Premium Mill Pond where he built a residence for his own use.

Rudy Schaeffer, whose father's home in Larchmont had been sold by us, decided to build a home in Pryer Manor for his own use.

The business executive, Mr. George B. Smith, a leader in the Ward Baking Company, bought a house which was being built by G. Richard Davis, the New York builder who had decided to build fine houses for sale in this district. Mr. John Hegeman, the New York building contractor, built a home for his own use.

The principal owners in the corporation, including myself, decided to each take several attractive plots and build homes of quality for

Anton L. Trunk Estate at Pryer Manor.

View of Pryer Manor from the Larchmont side.

sale. I picked two excellent sites and built such houses on them, which brings me to a very interesting experience. These two houses attracted the interest of a New York operator who owned a corner property in New York at 19th Street and Seventh Avenue. He offered to exchange this with me, and as I had been told that the New York real-estate operator Henry Mandel planned to create a new district of distinction in this Chelsea area, I decided to accept the offer of exchange. Later, Henry Mandel and I became friends, and he employed me to purchase some properties for him and eventually purchased the corner of Seventh Avenue and 19th Street from me. He was a man of great vision and courage, but suffered great losses in the 1929 depression.

CHAPTER VII

ALONG THE HUDSON

WHILE ALL THIS ACTIVITY was going on in the Larchmont area, our office was active in making sales in North Yonkers, Hastings, Greenburgh, Central and Northern Westchester up to Montrose Point near Peekskill. One of the sales which interested me greatly was the sale in 1919 of the estate of the noted writer Ralph Waldo Trine, known as Sunnybrae Farm on the Mount Airy Road at Croton-on-Hudson to Mumford S. Orth. (One of Mr. Trine's most popular books is "In Tune With The Infinite.") He was indeed a most interesting person to meet and do business with. This estate of his at Croton was on the top of high Mount Airy hill, commanding magnificent views of the surrounding country and the Hudson River.

With the development of the Harmon district below Croton, where all trains including expresses on the New York Central main line stopped to change engines, very rapid transportation to New York by express was available. Many very active business men of New York found it an excellent location for a country home, and it developed rapidly. Improvement of the Albany Post Road and plans which were under way to build parkways northward from New York through Upper Westchester and Putnam Counties were very stimulating. In a short time the Taconic Parkway and the Briarcliff-Croton Parkway were built. Among those attracted to the area north of Ossining were the famous actress Margaret Illington, and her husband, Major Edward Bowes, later famous for his radio program known as Major Bowes' Amateur Hour.

They were both extremely delightful in every way. They had a most attractive group of friends and entertained frequently at their charming home known as Dream Lake which they had created by modernizing and enlarging an old Colonial house in front of which they had made a lake, known as Dream Lake, by damming up an active brook. Their property contained many acres of land and was situated in an excellent district near Croton Lake. Nearby were several country places including the estate of actor Holbrook Blynn, known as Journey's End, overlooking a lake at the end of a long private road. Margaret Illington and her husband were close friends of Messmore Kendall, the New York lawyer who co-operated with Major Bowes in building the first large moving-picture theatre, known as the Capitol Theatre, on Broadway in New York City. General Coleman du Pont, a close friend of theirs and frequent visitor, was indeed a man of exceptional charm. He owned the old Waldorf Astoria Hotel at Fifth Avenue and 34th Street, and had taken a beautiful suite of rooms for his own use where he gave large parties, getting together a most delightful group of people.

Margaret Illington and Major Bowes became very good friends of mine and introduced me to many of their friends who became my clients. When they finally decided to sell their home, I found a purchaser for them in Arthur Geissler. I could write pages of many entertaining visits with this couple and their friends. After selling Dream Lake they bought a larger house on Croton Avenue in Ossining, and were among the most popular residents in this district.

he most attractive estate known as Dream ake, the home of Margaret Illington and Major Bowes.

A picture of Dream Lake.

White Plains

A sale in 1919 of which we were very proud was the sale of the magnificent estate known as Hillair, situated on Mamaroneck Avenue, White Plains. It was owned by Mrs. Mathilde E. Thebaud and sold to Armin Bencoe. This estate was on a hill commanding views of the surrounding country. It was one of the most beautiful and elaborate homes which had ever been built in Westchester County.

The sale of this estate frequently comes back to my mind. One day in the fall of 1919, when our business was very dull, Mr. Bencoe called at my office on Fifth Avenue and wanted to see me personally about buying a house. I was indeed glad to meet him. He told me that he had come to this country from Europe where he had been active in the sugar business and wanted a pleasant home in the suburbs. He asked whether it would be possible to go right out and look. My car was parked in the street in front of the office, and not having anything to keep me at the office, I said that I would be glad to go with him at once. On the way out he asked if we could stop at his hotel and pick up his wife. I said that I would be glad to do so. We drove to the hotel on Broadway near 70th Street, and when we picked up his wife we began to discuss their requirements.

I got the impression that they wanted a house of modest size and price, so when we reached the Scarsdale area I showed them a very attractive home of this type. When we stopped in front of the house

Main residence of estate known as Hillair belonging to Mathilde E. Thebaud.

they said that it was not big enough, they wanted something bigger. I then drove to a house somewhat larger. Again they said they wanted something bigger. After going from one house to another and having the same reply, I thought I would startle them by showing them the biggest house which we had listed. I drove up to the imposing entrance

Caretaker's cottage at entrance to the Thebaud Estate.

gate on Mamaroneck Avenue, White Plains, of the Thebaud mansion. To my surprise they seemed pleased. I had assumed that they would automatically say that it was too big. When I asked if they would like to see it, they said, "Of course." No one was residing there at the time. Due to war conditions, Mrs. Thebaud had moved into a much smaller house which she owned on the opposite side of Mamaroneck Avenue. So I said that we would have to go and get the key. When we arrived at Mrs. Thebaud's house, she answered the front door bell, and I told her that these people wanted to see Hillair, and asked for the key. I did not think the inspection would amount to anything, but thought I had better show it. She got the key and gave it to me. As I was leaving, Mr. Bencoe called out from the car, asking if she could not come along with us. She promptly agreed and came along with us.

We opened the huge outer iron-grille doors, then the massive oak doors and entered into a palatial hall. On one side was a French drawing room. A grand stairway led to the second floor. Large rooms, with French furniture, followed one after another. I noticed that Mr. and Mrs. Bencoe seemed very much interested, especially in the chandeliers and draperies. The more we looked the more serious they became. Finally, they asked the price. I thought it would scare them, even though it was only a fraction of the initial cost. This did not stun them. They then asked if they could also buy the furniture. Mrs. Thebaud said yes, and after some discussion named a price. After more looking and talking to one another in their language, they finally said they would take it. You could have knocked me down with a feather. The deal went through. Later, when they had moved in, they invited me and my wife to come to dinner, and they had engaged a fine cellist to play for us during dinner. They lived like kings of the old country. Some years later Mr. Bencoe transferred the house to a Wall Street operator, and I was told that he had suffered heavy financial losses. This is the property I sold later to Mr. Bert Herkimer to create the Saxon Woods Residential Park and Country Club.

Nearby was Gedney Farms, a suburban residential park where a splendid hotel with golf links had been developed. The whole White Plains area was in great demand. White Plains was the political center of Westchester County, and its business center was rapidly becoming one of the most important in the county.

Gedney Farms had been built as a residential park of the most distinguished type, and its hotel appealed to the most exacting taste. I remember spending several weeks there one summer, and in every way it was delightful. A few years later the hotel was completely destroyed by a disastrous fire. It was never rebuilt, and the neighborhood has never completely recovered from this loss.

The interest and enthusiasm which I developed in selling country estates to clients soon made me and my wife most anxious to find the ideal home for our own use. On the well-known Rocky Point in Old Greenwich a most interesting residence of Mediterranean architecture had been constructed. The property had a magnificent waterfront site and view, and was on a rocky shore without any sand beach, so that in order to go in swimming it was necessary to go out on a pier extending into deep water from which one could dive into the Sound. Among the many changes which I made in the house itself, which included an artistic patio, was the building of a tremendous swimming pool over the rocky shore with a high wall on the water side, two side walls and a wall at the end of our front lawn. A large inflow valve and pipe was installed where water could be drawn in at high tide and the valve closed off so as to provide excellent high tide swimming at all times. The bottom of this big pool consisted of a sandy bed so that swimming and wading in it was equal to the best facilities on the ocean beaches. If desired, the water could be changed with every change of tide.

Our family enjoyed the home very much indeed, but when we became interested in the White Mountains for summer vacation periods we rented the house to summer tenants. One of these was Mr. Lionel Noah who was the head of the American Woolen Company, and he and his wife during their summer tenancy became very much interested in acquiring the property, and after some negotiation I sold it to them. Mrs. Noah designed and created on the rear of the property a charming garden, which gained a great reputation and won prizes. A few years later everyone was greatly shocked by her death, and Mr. Noah finally decided to sell the property, which we did, to Mr. John C. Morrow.

Several years later, because of changes in his plans, Mr. Morrow authorized us to offer the place for sale, and we succeeded in selling it to Mr. John Schulte, who proceeded to embellish and beautify the property, and today it is an outstanding waterfront home.

Front view of former Howe residence overlooking Long Island Sound at Old Greenwich, Connecticut.

CHAPTER VIII

FURTHER DEVELOPMENT OF THE HUDSON RIVER DISTRICT

Now LET US COME BACK to our activities in the Hudson River district of Westchester. During the period of the first World War, the demand for country homes and the development of suburban areas had slowed down considerably, but as soon as the war was over the real-estate market improved. Better railroad transportation, the increase in the number of automobiles and the modernizing of the public roads made it increasingly easy for a business man with an office in New York to live in the country the year round. Ardsley Park, the charming suburban residential area north of Dobbs Ferry, with its highly rated golf club, came into prominence. Nearby was the famous St. Andrews Golf Club. Its golf course was said to be the first constructed in America. North of Ardsley was the village of Irvington-on-the-Hudson, which for many years had appealed to wealthy families who built large and luxurious estates creating a picture of country grandeur. North of Irvington was the village of Tarrytown, with its many historic spots, its famous schools, its scenic beauty and many other advantages. Many families located there, including that of John D. Rockefeller, who developed one of the largest and finest country estates in America.

Briarcliff and Vicinity

Beyond Tarrytown was the village of Briarcliff, where W. W. Law, one of the great men of his day, with wonderful imagination and creative foresight developed Briarcliff Manor, a residential district of merit. In its center he had built a country hotel, known as The Briarcliff Lodge, which had among its guests many notables of the time. Next to Briarcliff, the Sleepy Hollow Country Club had been organized. A golf course of the finest type had been built, and was widely acclaimed.

On one occasion while I was president of the Westchester Country Real Estate Board, a dinner was given by the Board to be held at Briarcliff Lodge. As the presiding officer, I knew that I would have to make a speech, and to add to the importance of the occasion I asked the secretary of the Board to ask Senator Chauncey DePew, who was residing at Briarcliff Lodge, to make an address. I knew that he had lived many years of his life near Peekskill and probably could give a most interesting address on a moment's notice. The secretary reported back that Senator DePew was willing, and as he was a humorist I thought of an interesting joke with which to introduce him. A number of years before, I had heard a joke about Senator DePew which I decided to repeat. It was as follows: On one occasion Senator DePew presided at a gathering where he was to introduce the noted orator Cyrus Northrup. When the time for introduction came, he arose and said that he was very happy indeed to have the honor of introducing Dr. Northrup who had done so much for the west and was famous as a wonderful orator. In fact he had become known as "the cyclone from the west." Dr. Northrup pretended to be offended and said that he did not know whether Senator DePew was giving him a compliment or not. It was the first time in his life that he had

Front entrance view of Briarcliff Lodge.

been called a cyclone, but if Senator DePew said it was so it must be so, as he was the greatest authority on winds in America.

When I gave Senator DePew this introduction he laughed and the audience roared. He gave us a very interesting address, naming many historical sites with which we were unfamiliar, which made northern Westchester history so fascinating. The dinner was indeed a success.

Mr. Robert Law, a son of the founder of Briarcliff, was then in charge of the Lodge and its extensive land holdings. He had heard of my success in organizing the Bonnie Briar Country Club in Larchmont, and asked me to organize a golf club on the Law property near the Briarcliff Lodge. A good golf club was needed as the only nearby club was the Sleepy Hollow Country Club, which had a waiting list. I took on the job and organized the Briar Hills Country Club. Devereux Emmet, who had designed the Bonnie Briar links in Larchmont, laid out the Briar Hills Golf course. It proved to be one of exceptional merit, and the club was a prompt success. I chose William J. Yates who was then connected with us to solicit members, and he did a great job.

In the Briarcliff district, William Rockefeller, the brother of John D. Rockefeller, had built a very large and handsome estate. Frank A. Vanderlip, the banker and philanthropist, Mr. R. T. Moore, E. S. Uhlman, Gustav Schwab, James Speyer, Helen Gibson, W. W. Fuller, V. Everett Macy, the founder of the Macy chain of newspapers, and many other families also built outstanding estates there. In many ways, Briarcliff was one of the leaders in the march of progress. It enjoyed a good commuting service from the Scarborough station on the main line of the New York Central Railroad, and also the Briarcliff station on the Putnam Division of the New York Central Railroad.

North of Briarcliff were Ossining, Harmon and Croton, which I have already described.

CHAPTER IX

CENTRAL WESTCHESTER

IN THE CENTRAL DISTRICT of Westchester our office was very active. Bronxville had been developed in two beautiful residential parks. One was Lawrence Park, east of the village and railroad station; and the other was Lawrence Park West, which was west of the railroad station. The Gramatan Hotel was just east of the station, and offered the best in hotel accommodations. My office was much impressed with the possibility of the profitable development of real estate in this district, and I organized a company with Lawrence Burrows and Elliot Ward as my associates, known as Burhoward, Inc. It took over from me a piece of property which I had previously purchased to build a co-operative apartment house at 64 Sagamore Road, a short distance from the Gramatan Hotel. We constructed this co-operative apartment house. It was somewhat ahead of the times, but it proved successful, and all the apartments were sold. The last apartment supplied a story of interest. Here it is:

View of the cooperative apartment at 64 Sagamore Road in Bronxville built by Burhoward, Inc.

Estates near Larchmont.

When we had sold all the apartments except one, we felt that it hardly paid to advertise one apartment for sale, so we decided to wait until a buyer came along in due course. One day I was busy in my office discussing the sale of an estate to important clients when Lawrence Burrows, my partner in Burhoward, Inc., came to the door and asked to see me for a minute. I left my desk and went over to talk to him. He said that there was a woman who wished to purchase the last apartment in 64 Sagamore Road, but she had a farm up in the White Mountains in New Hampshire which she wanted to trade for it. He didn't believe it amounted to much. Neither of us knew anything about the White Mountains and certainly would not ordinarily wish to buy a small farm there. However, we wanted to sell the apartment, and after a moment's thought I suggested that he get some cash from her and take the farm in exchange. We would probably be able to sell it through some local broker during the coming summer.

A few days later, he told me that he had sold the apartment to the lady, a Miss Edna Lewis, and would look to me to sell the farm. Well, time went on and we listed the property with the only broker we could locate in a nearby town. Nothing happened and and we became so busy with other ventures that Burhoward had undertaken, that the farm in New Hampshire was almost forgotten. When the modest taxes on the farm fell due, the secretary of the company would

make out a check, get Mr. Burrows to sign it, and he would incidentally remind me that he hoped I would find some way to sell it.

Again the matter drifted to the background. About a year later,
I had been so busy with many activities that I was dead tired, and
even though I had a home on the waterfront in Old Greenwich which
was a restful spot, I felt that I would like to go away for a vacation.
My wife thought it would be a fine idea. I told her that a friend of
mine had recently come back from a trip to the Mount Washington
Hotel in the White Mountains and was enthusiastic in his praise of it.
We decided the following week to take an automobile trip to the
Mount Washington Hotel.

The scenery on the way was wonderful, and we greatly enjoyed
it. The hotel proved to be even more wonderful than my friend had
described. On the first floor were spacious living rooms opening out
on wide porches which looked out over a beautiful golf course. Here
the women visited and played cards with one another while watching
the men playing golf. I ran into several friends and was introduced
to many other attractive people who were visiting there. I promptly
joined the golfers, and my wife joined the ladies. After several days,
my wife told me that I was neglecting her and ought to take her out
for a ride in this countryside. I agreed, and it suddenly occurred to
me that our Burhoward Comany may still have a farm somewhere
in the White Mountains, and it would be a good idea to go and take
a look at it if it was not too far away. I rang up the New York office
and was told that we still owned it and that it was known as Priscilla
Brook Farm near the village of Jefferson, New Hampshire. I asked
the hotel desk if they knew where Jefferson, New Hampshire, was and
they said it was over on U. S. Route 2 about 16 miles away on the
other side of Cherry Mountain, but there was a road over Cherry
Mountain which was fairly good, and I could go there without too
much trouble. I decided to do it, and soon we were on our way.

We reached Jefferson, a lovely little village with the famous
Waumbek Hotel and its cottages and golf course. There was a country
store with the post office at the main corner, and I thought that this
would be the best place to stop and ask questions. The storekeeper,
who was also the postmaster, was a very nice-looking fellow who,
when I asked him if he knew where Priscilla Brook Farm was,
promptly replied, "Sure, that was Miss Edna Lewis' place. She has
not been around for some time, and I believe that she sold it to some-
one." I asked how to get there, and he said to go down Route 2 for

about a mile to where there was a tea room. There I would see a
narrow road known as Ingerson Road which ran at right angles to
Route 2. Proceed on this road for about a mile until I came to a
bridge across a brook; that was Priscilla Brook, cross this bridge and
then I would see the Priscilla Brook Farm.

I promptly followed instructions, and as I drove along I saw the
most beautiful scenery imaginable, the whole White Mountain range
lined up across a beautiful valley. When I came to Priscilla Brook
and crossed the bridge, I saw a charming early American farmhouse
with lovely grounds and gardens, curtains in the windows. There was
a sign on the road in front of it reading Priscilla Brook Farm. I could
not believe that this was the place I was looking for, because it had
every sign of being well kept, while our farm had not been cared for,
for a long time. On the road beyond this was a red farm house which
looked neglected, so I felt that this must be our place. As I drove to
it I saw people on the front porch, and I assumed that they had taken
possession of the place as squatters because it was abandoned. However, I decided to stop and ask questions. A tall lanky fellow came
down from the porch to my car, and very politely and with a lovely
voice, which I later found was typical of people in the mountains,
asked me if there was anything he could do for me. I asked if he
knew where Priscilla Brook Farm was. He said, "You just passed it."
I said I meant a farm that Miss Lewis used to own. He repeated, "You
just passed it." I said that I could not believe that it was the place
as I was one of the owners and knew that nothing had been done for
two years to keep it up. He grabbed my hand and said, "Gee, I am
glad to meet you. Me and my wife have been looking after the place,
hoping that the owner would show up, as the greatest joy in my wife's
life is to see lights in that cottage at night. Don't you want to see it?
I have the key and will show you everything." My wife was listening
to all the talk, and said surely we would like to see it.

In the meantime the man, whose name was Seldon Ingerson, sum-
moned his wife and told her that here were the new owners of the
house. She was overjoyed. She said that she had been looking for us
for many days, and had everything in order for our arrival. Well, we
went into the house, Ingerson and his wife saying how they had kept
up the grounds for us, planted a garden, and had everything in readi-
ness for use. Sure enough, as we entered we found the furniture in
order, the curtains up, the kitchen with its stove and crockery ready
for use. I could not believe my eyes. I said to Mr. Seldon Ingerson,

My cottage on Priscilla Brook Farm in New Hampshire.

My former house in Brookside Park, Greenwich.

"Well, I must thank you for all the trouble you have taken; now I want to pay you. How much do I owe you?"

"Nothing," he said, "we are neighbors."

Well, I had to find ways of repaying him indirectly. Such is the character of these White Mountain natives. My wife took me to one side and said that it was silly to stay in a hotel when we had such a delightful spot to come to. I said that this was pioneering and would not be suitable for us on a vacation trip. The following summer my wife finally prevailed upon me to try the place for a summer visit. We had such a wonderful time, met such lovely neighbors, my wife found such interesting antique shops, that I decided to take the place over from our company and put it in her name. We used it as a summer cottage for many years, adding to it and making improvements until the year before my wife's death, when it was caught in the path of a West Indian hurricane which that year swept up from the south and destroyed many areas on the easterly end of Long Island and Connecticut, finally venting itself in the White Mountains. Just prior to the coming of the hurricane my wife and her sister, who had been visiting with her, planned to return from their summer vacation to New York. They had packed their belongings and driven in their car to say goodbye to their friends in neighboring estates and homes. As the wind increased in intensity, they decided to go back home, and in the distance they saw smoke coming through the trees. The closer they came to the house, the nearer the smoke appeared to the house itself, and finally when they crossed Priscilla Brook and came close to the house, they found one great blaze. The neighboring farmer had telephoned to the volunteer fire department, and many of them had come in haste to help. However, the fire was so intense and the wind so great that there wasn't the slightest chance of saving anything. The entire house and contents burned to the ground. This was a tremendous shock to my wife, and her sister noticed that she must be seriously ill. She promptly got our local doctor, and he decided that my wife had better immediately go over to the nearby home of the Wilds who had volunteered their aid, and be placed in bed as she was unable to speak and seemed to be in complete shock. They got me on the phone in New York, and I immediately went to the mountains to see what I could do to help. After several days, my wife improved sufficiently for me to take her back to the city, but the shock had done such damage to her health that several months later she had a cerebral hemorrhage and died.

After the fire, I tried to determine its cause as no stoves or lights had been left burning in the house when my wife and her sister left to visit friends, and the fire insurance expert asked me if any open box of matches had been left in the kitchen. It seemed that a large box of wooden matches had been left open on the kitchen table under curtains at the windows. It developed that field mice during bad weather manage to get into houses and, as they are very fond of matches, if any are around they proceed to gnaw at them. The decision of the experts was that a mouse had gotten into the house, gotten on the kitchen table, had seen the open box of matches and proceeded to eat them and thus caused them to blaze up and the whole box caught on fire. This fire reached the curtains on the windows, and with the high wind that was blowing a terrific fire immediately occurred. I mention this as it may be helpful information to others who do not know of this tendency of field mice. In this case it brought on a real tragedy.

CHAPTER X

SCARSDALE AREA—NORTHERN WESTCHESTER

NORTH OF BRONXVILLE, the area around the village of Scarsdale was beginning to bloom, stimulated greatly by the genius and skill of Robert E. Farley and Stephen L. Angell. Fox Meadow, which has since become an outstanding suburban residential park, was then undeveloped land.

When the Bronx River Parkway was opened, the entire countryside on both sides of this parkway screamed with delight. It was indeed a great achievement. The Westchester Park Commission which planned and brought it into existence, encouraged by its success, proceeded to develop the famous parkway system of Westchester County. This made the whole country an accessible residential area of the best type.

One of the sales in which I was interested in the early months of 1916, was a tract of vacant land containing about 60 acres, situated at the corner of the Fort Hill Road and Central Avenue in Yonkers, not far from Scarsdale. This property was being offered at a very reasonable price, and I considered it a good investment. Together with one of my closest friends and associates, Robert T. Wood, whom I have always considered one of our ablest lawyers, I organized a company known as Central Park Avenue Estates, Inc., and purchased the property.

I could envision a very large development of homes of modest size and price because of its location in the town of Yonkers. However, we were busy in many other directions at the time, and the opportunity presented itself to exchange it on advantageous terms for a waterfront estate belonging to Charles S. Thorne in West Islip, Long Island, which we thought could be resold in a short time. We closed the deal and resold the Long Island property the following spring. Mr. Thorne, who originally intended to use the Central Avenue property, because of a change of plans sold it to Mr. Fred Fox, a real-estate operator who sold a large part of it to a developer who constructed roads and successfully built houses of the type which I had originally envisioned. Much of the adjoining land was similarly developed. When I ride through the various streets and see this very extensively built-up area, and then ride down to Central Avenue in front of it and see the luxurious suburban restaurant of Patricia Murphy, the many stores, and garden apartments nearby I find it hard to realize that a few years ago it was vacant land.

Central Avenue grew very rapidly after it was widened all the way to White Plains. It is now a main road from New York to White Plains, and the area on both sides of it has become a business highway.

Chappaqua

North of Scarsdale, were Hartsdale and White Plains. Beyond White Plains, one enters the beautiful country of Northern Westchester where our office had been increasingly busy. We made many sales in this area and took a very interesting part in its development. In fact, I became so much impressed with the opportunity for develop-

Herzig Estate in Armonk, sold to Mr. Sarnoff.

ment which I saw in the little village of Chappaqua, a few miles north of White Plains, that I decided to take a very active part in its progress. Here Horace Greeley, editor of The New York Tribune, had built his estate. Later, A. H. Smith, then president of the New York Central Railroad, had acquired a large acreage and built a magnificent country home. The railroad station at Chappaqua and its surroundings were rural and attractive. Adjoining it was a large area which belonged to the Greeley estate and had never been developed. Beyond this was a very small business district. On approaching Chappaqua, one felt that one was really in the country. Great hills and rolling land higher than anything south of it made a beautiful landscape. The high and dry air made the year-round climate pleasant and healthful.

I envisioned the creation of an attractive village center, and with my associates in Burhoward, Inc. we bought from the Greeley estate a large part of the land on both sides of Greeley Avenue, a business street which ran parallel to the railroad track several hundred feet east of the railroad station. I personally bought from Wilbur Hyatt, the father of one of my very able associates, Schuyler M. Hyatt, business property which he owned at the corner of Greeley Avenue and Main Street, which then housed the town clerk's office. Burhoward, Inc. proceeded to design a store building with a number of stores. The corner store was for a bank which we hoped could be organized because we believed that Chappaqua needed a bank. We were fortunate in encouraging Mr. Jackson Chambers, then president of the Gramatan National Bank and Trust Company in Bronxville, to take an interest in this plan, and he organized the Chappaqua National

The estate of Horace Greeley in Chappaqua, New York.

rt of the Greeley Estate on Greeley Avenue, Chappaqua.

Part of the Greeley Estate developed by Mr. Howe on King Street, Chappaqua.

Bank, which rented our corner store. It is interesting to note that this bank grew and grew until it is now highly rated. It is no longer a tenant. In due course it bought the building from us and has enlarged it.

Most of the land between Greeley Avenue and the railroad station is now owned by the town and is a park with fine trees and extensive parking facilities for commuters. When the passengers on a railroad train look out of the car windows when the train stops at Chappaqua they see an ideal suburb. On the land which I personally purchased, I built a store building which includes among its tenants the Chappaqua Post Office, a large grocery store, a Rexall Drug Store, a liquor store and our real-estate office.

The great hill-top estates surrounding the Village of Chappaqua in the early days included the Bristol Estate, the McKesson estate, the Neustadt estate, the Turner estate, the Guinzburg estate, the A. H. Smith estate, the Greeley estate and many others. As time has gone on, many of these estates have been subdivided into charming residential districts. Nearby one sees the Chappaqua Public High School which rates as one of the finest in the county. In fact, the public schools of Chappaqua have been a strong attraction for many families with children, seeking suburban homes.

It was natural for me to stop a while in my story to talk about Chappaqua, but I will now continue my description of the rapid

View of Chappaqua and Greeley Avenue in its early days before the town was developed.

Present day view of Greeley Avenue shown in picture
No. 1.

growth of the other districts in North Central Westchester, including
Pleasantville, Mount Kisco, Bedford, Katonah, the Salems, all the
way to Brewster and beyond into Putnam and Dutchess Counties. To

show how hard we worked and what a wide area we studied, as far back as November, 1919, Mr. Schuyler Hyatt sold a farm estate, belonging to J. W. Charlton, in North Salem on the edge of Ridgefield, Connecticut, containing approximately 54 acres, to Samuel Bird, for use as a year-round gentleman's farm and country home. At about the same time, we sold the charming country home of E. Louis Tewksbury, situated on the Whippoorwill Road in Chappaqua, to Henry L. Glazier of New York. This property is on a ridge commanding extensive views.

At about this time, we also made a sale which was the opening event in what later became the sale of an extensive area to the developers of one of the most attractive residential parks near Chappaqua. The property which I am referring to was owned by Anna W. McKay, and it was situated on what had always been known as the Whippoorwill Road, and contained 340 acres of land with a number of residences. The sale was made to one of our clients, Mr. F. A. Russell, for investment. After holding the property for about a year, Mr. Russell succeeded in interesting Mr. Frederick Ruth, a most extraordinary real-estate developer, who decided to buy the property and much adjoining acreage.

A real-estate development was created by Mr. Ruth which he named the Whippoorwill Country Club and Park. He had earned great fame already by having developed the outstanding residential park at Lake Wales, in Florida, known as the Mountain Lake Club, consisting of large orange groves and a residential area to which he invited families of importance to become club members and residents. None of his property was offered for sale in the market through real-estate brokers. He personally invited chosen families to visit his property as guests, and if everything worked out as planned, he invited them to become residents. His plan was very successful, and he made a similar development at Fisher's Island on Long Island Sound. The district around Chappaqua appealed to him, and on the large tract of land on Whippoorwill Road which he had purchased, he planned and organized the Whippoorwill Country Club with beautiful roads and a fine golf course. Many outstanding citizens promptly became members, and homes of great value were built. The owner of one of these estates which we later listed for sale told me that he had spent $500,000 in construction and equipment. This gives an indication of what grandeur existed in Whippoorwill.

CHAPTER XI

UPPER HUDSON AREA

ONE OF OUR OUTSTANDING EARLY SALES in Upper Westchester was the sale of the gentleman's farm estate of D. R. Hanna, situated in the town of Yorktown north of Ossining, to Gerard Swope, who was president of the General Electric Company. Mr. Hanna, a relation of the political leader Mark Hanna, had developed this large estate to such a point that it had few equals. One of our office associates, Mr. William J. Yates, succeeded in selling the property to Mr. Swope, and this stood out as quite a real-estate achievement.

In the early twenties I began to go down to Florida for winter vacations, and one of the places of greatest popularity and attraction was Miami Beach where Carl Fisher the real-estate genius, had created a resort of great beauty and ideal enjoyment. A visitor from the northern cold climates could go by train and find himself the

Main residence on the Gerard Swope Estate in Yorktown near Ossining.

next day in a delightful summer atmosphere where he could have a fine swim in water of mild temperature. I registered at a pleasant hotel on the ocean front and had the good fortune of becoming friends with Mr. and Mrs. E. C. Sams who were staying there. He was the president of the J. C. Penney Company which operated a chain of stores throughout the country. Mr. Sams and I played golf frequently, and he introduced me to Mr. J. C. Penney, who had built a beautiful estate on one of the Venetian Islands on Venetian Way, an avenue leading across Miami to Miami Beach. We all played golf together from time to time, along with Mr. Harvey Firestone of Firestone Tire, who had an estate on the ocean front at Miami Beach.

One day, Mr. Penney, Mr. Sams, Mr. Firestone and myself, had arranged to have a golf game, but when we arrived at the golf links Mr. Penney was not there. This was surprising because he was always punctual. After waiting a while we started to play, leaving word for him to join us on the course when he arrived. We had gone just a few holes when a message from Mr. Penney came saying that his wife had died suddenly. We, of course, all went over to his house to help in any way we could. Mr. Penney was prostrated. His wife was a lovely woman, and he was deeply shocked and saddened.

Emmadine Farm, the farm estate of J. C. Penney in Hopewell Junction.

As time went on, Mr. Sams told me that he was very much worried about Mr. Penney's health and that we would have to try to find some hobby or interest that would take his mind off his worries. Mr. Sams said that he thought maybe some kind of farm activity would be the answer. I said that I would see Mr. Penney and suggest that he acquire a farm. He was won over to the plan. Our Mr. Yates showed him a farm near Hopewell Junction, Dutchess Country, known as Emmadine Farm. It contained many hundred acres of land with farm buildings and was an excellent place to raise cattle. He bought the farm, and several weeks later I met him on Fifth Avenue near my office. He said that he was just coming over to see me. He pulled out

The beautiful Ralph Harris Estate in Somers.

of his pocket some attractive pictures of cattle, including the picture of a magnificent bull, and asked me what I thought of the bull. Of course I said it was wonderful. "Well," he said, "I just bought it. That is the picture of Langwater Foremost, the finest Guernsey bull in existence. I have hired an excellent farmer and breeder, and plan to develop a new strain of Guernsey cows. Most of them in this country now are sickly and not very strong. I plan to go to the Island of Guernsey and buy the best strong, healthy cows with straight backs, good chests, good udders and bring them to this country and breed them to Langwater Foremost. Watch this and see the results."

Mr. Penney did develop a new strain known as Foremost Guernseys, now the leading strain of Guernsey. He enjoyed having me visit

Emmadine Farm from time to time, showing me the remarkable results of his efforts. Out of this extraordinary achievement, besides the outstanding breed of cattle known as Foremost Guernseys, came the present extensive Emmadine Dairy Farm Stores, and the nationwide Foremost Dairy Company. All of this goes to show how an unforeseen incident sometimes develops to such a size as to make history.

Westchester Hills

About this time we sold a very attractive place (situated in the Town of Somers, Westchester County, just beyond Pinesbridge which crosses Croton Lake) to James R. Brown. The property contained an extensive acreage, and the site where the residence was located commanded grand views. We always looked upon it as one of the most interesting sites in this section of Westchester County. Several years later a New York lawyer, Henry J. Bigham, was looking for an estate with a house of modest size and extensive acreage. After much searching, he decided to purchase through us the Brown property which had come on the market, and after taking possession he made extensive improvements in the house and surrounding land and bought a large additional acreage. It is interesting to note that at a later date Mr. John Ritchie, who was the head of the Fifth Avenue Coach Company, inquired at our office about country places in Westchester, and when we showed this property of Mr. Bigham to Mr. and Mrs. Ritchie, they immediately became very much attached to it, and we promptly made a sale to Mr. Ritchie who lived there for many years.

In 1922, Mr. Schuyler Hyatt took one of our clients, Mr. Edmund C. Vaughan, through the various estates in the Bedford and Katonah area of Westchester County. Mr. Hyatt had often discussed with me the many beauties of the Thorne Estate on which a house of exceptional merit had been constructed and which had been developed as a practical farm estate. Mr. Vaughan was much attracted to the property, and after some negotiations, Mr. Hyatt succeeded in making the sale to him. Shortly afterwards he bought an adjoining property, which made it a most interesting and beautiful estate where the Vaughans made their permanent home.

About this time, the area around Armonk and North Castle was becoming very popular with the improvement of Route 22 which made travel to this district easy. Dr. Charles Paterno, who later was one of our important clients in the Greenwich area, had bought a large tract of land on Route 22 and developed a farm known as

Windmill Farm because he dug many artesian wells on the property which were operated by picturesque windmills. Dr. Paterno was an extraordinary man in every way. He loved to build stone walls, plant tree nurseries and create lakes. On Windmill Farm he created lakes, filling them with water pumped up by these numerous windmills. The place was one of great interest all during his life, and now has been developed into a fine suburban residential park.

We sold to Albert J. Stone, the railroad executive, the F. M. Tompkins, the S. R. Close and the Lester Wilson properties near Windmill Farm. He took much interest in the real-estate activities in this district. Mr. Schuyler Hyatt had originally made the sale to Mr. Stone of the Tompkins property and had told me what a very fine couple he and his wife were. After moving into the Close estate he bought the Wilson property as an investment. Before he took title to the Wilson property, the house burned down, and a problem of how to share the loss and the insurance developed, but was finally amicably settled. He was a man of exceptional ability, and I had the pleasure of meeting him and having many very interesting talks with him. He had been a leading executive of the Erie Railroad before he had retired. From his long experience in business, he told me, he believed firmly in the soundness and desirability of real-estate investments. This made me feel very good, as it was one of my arguments on many occasions when selling desirable properties to clients.

The building of the Saw Mill River Parkway and other parkways brought a very rapid increase in the population of Northern Westchester, and before 1930 it had become a highly developed suburban area in sharp contrast with the preceding farm period.

CHAPTER XII

ALONG THE SOUND

OUR OFFICE IN LARCHMONT was full of energy and activity. We were successful in selling the beautiful Alice C. Dickerman estate on Weaver Street in Larchmont to Louis Guinzburg. One of our clients at this time was Vivian Green, who had been very successful as a New York real-estate operator. He wanted to buy a country home for his own use, and as he inspected various properties he developed the desire to create a very fine suburban residential park where he could have his own house surrounded by lovely suburban homes, preferably on the shore of Long Island Sound. To find an ideal location was quite a problem, but we finally sold him the Richard Ricker estate right on the boundary line between Rye and Mamaroneck facing Long Island Sound. Here he developed the outstanding suburban residential district known as Greenhaven.

Later he acquired additional surrounding acreage which he beautified and developed with ever-increasing charm and quality. Greenhaven became the leading and most desired section in the nearby suburbs on Long Island Sound. We helped in its planning and took great pride in the final result. It includes all the land between the Boston Post Road and Long Island Sound bounded on the east side by Barlow Lane and on the west by Greenhaven Avenue. Van Amringe Mill Pond is on the west side with a tidal dam at its entrance, supplying an attractive lake front area with high water at all tides. Greenhaven Harbor, between the mainland and Hen Island on the South side, provides a shore frontage safe from damage by high waves in storms, also excellent beach club bathing facilities.

Vivian Green was indeed a developer who combined not only great imagination but also exceptional practical judgment and good taste. He would sit for hours with me on weekends, outlining his plans and asking what had been done in other exclusive suburban parks where we had had considerable experience. He adopted the plan of having an architectural and construction department to design houses for buyers of plots and also to design and build some lovely homes for sale. His own home on the waterfront was a work of art. We had occasion to interest many of our clients in this property and have

Residence of Vivian Green overlooking Long
Island Sound at Greenhaven.

The estate of Carl Loeb acquired by Albe
Warner overlooking Long Island Sound
Rye, New York.

made sales of the fine homes there, and can say without hesitation
that Greenhaven has retained top rank.

Another developer who became my very good friend and client
appeared on the scene at this time. He was Bert Herkimer, a New York
lawyer, who had become interested in suburban home development.
He started in Pelham and was very successful. I met him as a result
of selling properties in Pelham and found that he was looking for
more land to develop, and we promptly made an extensive search for
suitable property. Finally he chose the Rhodes property, running
through from Weaver Street, Larchmont, to Griffen Avenue, and here
he developed an attractive subdivision which proved successful. We
sold him adjoining land on which he organized a golf club.

About this time the Hutchinson River Parkway was being laid
out, and it took some of the land originally planned for the golf course,

pical residence in Broadmoor development
Bert Herkimer on Weaver Street in Scarsdale area near Larchmont.

The beautiful estate of Harry Winston on Old
Mamaroneck Road, Scarsdale.

so he acquired additional land to take its place. Shortly afterwards,
Mr. Herkimer arranged through me to purchase the Osborne estate
at the foot of Barry Avenue in Shore Acres, Mamaroneck, where he
organized a beach and shore club of great charm. With these achievements to his credit, he planned a larger undertaking, and I sold him
the former Thebaud mansion in White Plains, which we had some
years previously sold to Armin Bencoe. In addition to the Thebaud
estate he purchased adjoining acreage. He then designed and developed the beautiful Saxon Woods Country Club, using the mansion
and horse stables for a riding club which attracted many members.
The land was subdivided into building sites on which many handsome
houses were built.

Unfortunately, the 1929 depression came. He had spent large
sums and made many commitments to carry out his project successfully, but had not yet had time to make sufficient sales to meet his
obligations. The result was that Herkimer lost this development which
eventually was carried on by others.

Of the many sales of outstanding estates which my office made
in the Larchmont area in the early days, one of the most important
which we were very proud of was the sale in October, 1919, of the
beautiful residence of Albert Steiglitz, situated on Weaver Street on
a large acreage site, to Mr. Mercadante. This property was not far

from the entrance to Larchmont Gardens and added greatly to the attractiveness of the neighborhood.

Shortly after this, we decided to open an office in Rye and selected a location on the Boston Post Road in the center of the town where we constructed a real-estate office. This proved successful and encouraged us to open an office on the Boston Post Road in Greenwich a year later, with Marshall Allaben as manager. We promptly became active in the sale of properties in Greenwich, Stamford and the nearby Connecticut area. These districts were growing rapidly. I witnessed many achievements. Among them, I might mention a sale in February of 1922. Mr. R. H. Arnold was making an extensive search for a lovely site in Greenwich where he could build a model house. We were offering for sale at that time a tract of land situated on Lake Avenue through which ran a very attractive brook. Beyond this brook the land rose rapidly to a high ridge commanding beautiful views. The property was owned by the well-known student of nature, J. Thompson Seton, who on several occasions had outlined its charms to me. Mr. Allaben showed this property to Mr. Arnold and succeeded in making a sale of 13 acres on which Mr. Arnold proceeded to build one of the most attractive homes in the Greenwich area.

In the Rye area John Mc. E. Bowman acquired the great Park Estate, and with an imagination and energy which knew no bounds planned and carried through to completion the finest combination of a residential park and country club in this country which he named the Westchester Biltmore Country Club. It consisted of a club building with all the facilities and services of a palatial hotel, and three golf courses. Beautiful avenues were laid out with many exceptionally attractive building sites on which luxurious country homes were built. Shortly afterwards, the club acquired a large waterfront site adjoining Manursing Island on Long Island Sound where a beach club of the finest type was developed. These wonderful additions to the community brought Rye into great prominence, and drew many families to the area for their year-round homes.

I live there myself at the present time, and must say that the Westchester Country Club is without an equal anywhere. Bowman, when he dreamed of its creation, spent fabulous sums of money and certainly provided fabulous facilities. When the 1929 depression came, Bowman and all his hotels took the count. Finally the members of the Westchester Biltmore Country Club joined hands and took it over from the mortgagee for a fraction of its cost. The name was changed from the Westchester Biltmore Country Club to the West-chester Country Club. To provide similar facilities in a new club today would cost several times what Bowman spent. It can be readily seen that today no one would even try to build a similar club.

One of our most conspicuous sales in this district was the mag-nificent waterfront estate on Milton Point, which was owned by Carl Loeb, a New York financier. This property was a waterfront castle. It was situated on Forest Avenue in a section of Milton Point enjoying not only beach facilities but with an inlet which provided safe anchorage for boats. It was screened from Forest Avenue by a high stone wall. The house itself was tremendous. Its original cost was said to have been more than $1,000,000. When Mr. Loeb purchased it, he improved it in many ways. Finally he and his wife decided that it was larger than they needed and offered it for sale. I was one of the fortunate brokers who had it listed. One day one of my clients rang me up and told me that Albert Warner, a friend of his who had made a great fortune as a moving picture pioneer, had mentioned that he would like to get a place in the country. I got in touch with Mr. Warner.

He and his wife were lovely people. They made several trips of inspection with me, but after listening to their requirements I hesitated to show them the Loeb estate which was so big. However, as a final chance I took them into the Loeb estate. The weather was fine, and the outlook over Long Island Sound was compelling. As I took them through the house, they seemed pleased. I heard Mr. Warner ask his wife if it was big enough. She answered that they entertained a great deal, and she thought it might do. Finally Mr. Warner asked me what Mr. Loeb wanted for it. I had not mentioned price for fear that it would kill the deal at once. When I did mention it, he consulted with his wife and suggested that I offer Mr. Loeb a figure very close to what he wanted. I was thrilled. Mr. Loeb did not enthuse but went off and discussed the matter with his wife, and then returned telling me that he had decided to take it. I called both parties together, told them that they had made a purchase and sale, and had them shake hands on the deal. Knowing both parties, I knew that this was as sure a deal as if each had put up a million dollars. Their words were their bonds, and contracts and title closings followed in due course.

Not to be outdone by Rye, our Greenwich office was now playing a leading role in its field. We were one of the organizers of the Maremount Corporation which developed a section of Mead's Point.

Later we were appointed exclusive brokers for the sale of the very luxurious country estate of Gustave Schwab which was sold by Ladd and Nichols to Mr. Zalmon G. Simmons, the head of the Simmons Company, makers of Simmons beds. Our office made many other sales, including the estate of E. L. Rossiter to Ralph Worthington, and the June Sturges waterfront estate, situated on Steamboat Road near the Indian Harbor Yacht Club, to Mr. Otis A. Kenyon of Kenyon, Eckhardt Inc:, a leading New York advertising agency.

At about this time our Chappaqua office was also very active. Mr. Hyatt of that office showed a beautiful property situated at Golden's Bridge, belonging to Charlotte Cannon, to Miss Elizabeth A. Allen, one of our special clients. She was looking for a property with magnificent views in a very rural area. The property that he showed her happened to contain two main residences, both of which had good views, and a farm cottage with farm buildings and many acres of lovely land including a private lake. The property interested her so much that she finally bought it with the intention of selling off part of the land and one of the main houses and possibly the farm cottage. After extensive alterations and decoration, both of these additional houses were sold by our office, and we were very much pleased. Miss Allen had been a prominent actress, and of course the sale gave us some very pleasant publicity.

We made one sale in 1924 which stood out in our records. It was one of the beautiful residences on the estate of the late E. C. Converse, one of the close associates of the late Andrew Carnegie in the steel industry. When the steel corporation was sold to the J. P. Morgan interests by Mr. Carnegie, he and Mr. Converse retired. Mr. Converse finally decided to accumulate a large acreage in Greenwich, Connecticut, where he constructed a palatial stone mansion, two additional smaller mansions, a number of farm buildings for the raising of cattle, very large orchards of apples and other fruits, with the necessary buildings for their storage and sale. Finally he built a dam, creating a lake known as Converse Lake and a lake house and dock. The property included about 800 acres of land in Greenwich, and extended over into Westchester County in New York with almost as many additional acres. With its roads and facilities it was famous and considered one of the finest estates in the New England states. When Mr. Converse died the property finally was placed on the market by the Bankers Trust Company of New York. Our office made one of the first sales. We sold one of the houses on the property with about ten acres of land to Mr. C. E. Knickerbocker. This was the beginning of our good fortune in connection with this estate. Later we sold the property for Mr. Knickerbocker to Howard R. Platt. I will tell more later about the Converse estate.

Shortly after World War I, in 1919, Mr. Sol Bloom called at our office and advised us that he had a client, Mrs. Delia L. Martin, a widow, who was looking for property in the hills north of Stamford, Connecticut, where she and her married son could enjoy a farm estate of size. One of my co-operating brokers in Stamford, G. Harry Abbott, and I had often discussed the many fine estates which he was offering for sale in that area. I requested his co-operation in finding a suitable place for Mrs. Martin. After very extensive inspection trips, Mrs. Martin finally selected a property known as Rippowam Lodge which was situated on Stillwater Avenue and Roxbury Road extending back to West Hill Road, containing a large acreage on which there was an attractive colonial residence together with barns and other outbuildings. This investment proved to be a most successful one in every way. The Martins used the property for many years. The development of Stamford since then brought about extensive subdivision and development of the land in this area, including the Martin farm. There are now a great many homes located on the property, and a portion of it situated on Roxbury Road has been acquired by the City of Stamford for the public school known as the Roxbury School.

CHAPTER XIII

GREENWICH, STAMFORD AND VICINITY

THE SALE OF RIPPOWAM LODGE FARM impressed me with the future of real-estate development in Stamford which was called the Lock City because the Yale and Town Manufacturing Company, the leading manufacturers of locks, was located there and had done much to make it a highly rated business center.

In the area near the Stamford railroad station on South Street, the Yale and Town Manufacturing Company had acquired the Ferguson estate and constructed on a part of it one of the first garden apartments to be erected in the suburbs. They planned it originally for the use of company employees. The plan included a large two-story garden apartment house laid out like a tremendous square with a large open area in the center. Its front resembled a group of attached private houses, each with two separate apartments, one on the first and one on the second floor. Each apartment had its own front entrance door and its own rear door leading to its own private backyard. Each had its own part of the cellar with its own heating system so that each tenant supplied his own heat. In addition, there was an attractive park in the enclosed center area back of the private backyards of individual tenants, where all tenants and their children could enjoy themselves. The original apartment house occupied about one-fourth of the land of the Ferguson estate, and it was probably the original intention of the company to build additional apartments on the balance of the land. The entire project was called Rippowam Village, because it bordered on the Rippowam River.

Changes in plans decided the company to sell the entire development. As before stated, I had great confidence in the future of Stamford, and when the Yale and Town Manufacturing Company offered Rippowam Village for sale, I discussed the matter with my associates in the Burhoward Company and we decided to buy Rippowam Village from Yale and Town and continue the development of the property. This we did, and shortly afterwards built a four-story apartment house on a part of the property.

In due course, we sold the property for business and residential use, and for years it was a pleasing site near the Stamford station, but as often happens the best laid schemes of mice and men gang aft a-gley. The development of roads and parkways to serve the needs of transportation brought about the construction of the New England Thruway. It was planned and finally built, and now includes a large part of Rippowam Village, including the apartment houses. These were taken over and demolished by the Parkway Authority. The Thruway now rides proudly over the site.

Another of our real-estate sales which stands out in my memory, was the sale in 1928 of the estate of Dr. Robert Morris to the Storm Holding Company. George Storm, a New York lumber dealer who lived in Greenwich, conceived the idea of purchasing a large tract of land extending from Cognewaugh Road in Greenwich to Westover Road in Stamford for a large development project. The area which he chose consisted of many hundreds of acres through which the Mianus River ran. It included a number of different units with different owners. One of the large tracts extending to Westover Road in Stamford was owned by Dr. Morris who occupied a country residence on the property with an entrance on Westover Road. The entire area all the way over to Cognewaugh Road in Greenwich was beautiful woodland through which bridle paths had been laid out, providing a charming area for horseback riding. Mr. Storm was a horseman and had often ridden there. He requested my office to find out whether the owners of the various tracts would be willing to sell and, if so, at what prices. We knew that Dr. Morris would be willing to sell, but as to the other owners we would have to find out. We proceeded on this task with care and patience. Dr. Morris, after much negotiation, finally agreed on a price and terms which were accepted by Mr. Storm, and the property was sold to the Storm Holding Company. After considerable effort, we finally purchased for Mr. Storm and his associates the remaining acreage which he desired. One tract facing Mianus River belonged to the Havemeyer estate, and we considered ourselves very fortunate when we brought about this sale, as the Havemeyer land holdings had been purchased for investment and were not then being offered for sale.

We were also proud of the sale of the beautiful estate on Ponus Ridge in the north end of Stamford on the border of New Canaan, for Gayer Dominick, a partner in the brokerage firm of Dominick and Dominick, to Edward Plaut, the president of Lehn and Fink

Products Corporation. This house was one of the finest in the Connecticut area.

I had often inspected and discussed the property with Mr. Dominick, and considered it one of the most attractive that we were offering for sale. The house itself was a gem of architecture situated on a high elevation approached by a beautiful driveway, commanding views of the surrounding country. It was of ample size for very gracious living. On the grounds were excellent horse stables, several cottages and other farm buildings. Adjoining were beautiful bridle paths. It was a horseman's paradise. Mr. Plaut was an enthusiastic horseman and bought the property.

He then added improvements and embellishments, including a most luxurious swimming pool. Several years later when Mr. Plaut, because of change of plans, decided to sell the property, I showed it to Mr. and Mrs. Thomas J. Watson. Mr. Watson was the president of the International Business Machines Company and one of the greatest business leaders of our times. He had a great knowledge of real estate throughout the country, and he and his wife admired the Plaut estate. After some negotiation I succeeded in bringing about a sale to him. He used it as a summer home for many years.

Another sale with which I was well pleased, was the sale in 1927 of the waterfront estate of Thomas J. O'Rourke, situated on a large waterfront acreage at Cummings Point in Stamford, to Willis G. McCullough, New York industrialist. The sale was made in co-operation with Douglas Elliman and Company of New York. This property was one of the most exceptional waterfront estates on the north shore of Long Island Sound within commuting distance of New York City.

It included a very large acreage within easy reach of the Stamford and Old Greenwich stations on the New Haven Railroad. A point of land extended into the Sound, so that a good safe harbor for boats could be built with lovely shore-front facilities and guest cottages. Mr. McCullough, who was a man of wealth, proceeded at once to do extensive dredging, to build a harbor and dock for large yachts and a beautiful sand bathing beach of considerable length. He made the acreage back of the residence into a productive farm. The main residence itself was made into a luxurious year-round home. He was deeply in love with the property, and every time I visited him he grew more eloquent in its praise, which increased my joy for having made the sale.

Next to the McCullough estate, Mr. Francis L. Field had

developed the peninsula in Stamford known as South Field Point, where he had created a high-class suburban residence park, including an exceptional private school which attracted many important families. As time went on, Mr. Field, who was devoting his entire time to the project, became interested in other business in New York City and desired to sell to some developer who would take over the project. He discussed the matter with me at length.

Apartment house opposite railroad station in
Larchmont.

It happened that one of our clients was a builder of a number of apartment houses in New Rochelle, Larchmont and Mamaroneck. The market for apartment houses was very quiet at the time, and the thought occurred to me that I might get this builder to take over the South Field Point development in part-payment for one of his apartment houses, if I could get Mr. Field interested. After extensive negotiations, I finally brought about an exchange of Mr. Field's interest in South Field Point for an apartment house situated on Palmer Avenue, Larchmont, an excellent location near the Larchmont railroad station.

In the fall of 1927, I had the pleasure of meeting a Wall Street broker, Mr. Howard Eric, member of the firm of Eric and Drevers, who told me that he would like to buy a country home in a location where he could commute easily. The house was to be a genuine early American, where he could keep horses and have good bridle paths. He also wanted excellent fields, lovely woodland, an active brook, and a lake for fishing and water sports.

After hearing his description, I told him that he was describing a property, belonging to Mrs. B. Goulden, which had recently come on the market on the Riverbank Road in Stamford. He and his wife inspected the property with me, and they naturally fell in love with it and bought it. With exquisite taste and imagination they added to it and made it one of the most attractive country homes near New York. They lived in it for many years until the death of Mr. Eric, after which we sold it to Mr. and Mrs. Irving Kraunz, who again added to its charm and enjoyed it for a number of years. Later when they offered it for sale due to a change in their plans, we sold it to one of New York's real-estate leaders, Mr. Edward Benenson, and his wife. They also added to its beauty, and reside there now.

One of my most pleasant reminiscences is in connection with W. Stewart Thompson, the architect, who is widely known for the many outstanding buildings which he has designed, including university buildings in Athens, Greece. Mr. Thompson had been chosen by Mrs. H. W. Nuckols to design the magnificent home which she built on a large tract of land on the Stanwich Road in North Greenwich. The sightliness of the location appealed to him and his wife, and he acquired a parcel of this land from Mrs. Nuckols and built a very unique and attractive home for his own use. At a later date, one of my clients, Walter Lagemann, was searching for a house. Mr. Thompson's place seemed to fit his requirements exactly. I succeeded in bringing about a sale, and Mr. Lagemann added additional wings, a large entrance patio for cars bringing guests to his house, a tennis court, and other buildings.

In the meanwhile, Mr. Thompson developed a strong urge to purchase land for subdivision and building exceptional homes for sale. After some search I sold him a tract of land in the Hill Crest Park Section of Greenwich which was being offered for sale by the Chase National Bank of New York, and he subdivided the property which was in a highly considered district and built a number of houses, all of which he sold. This kindled his desire for subdivision and building, and I later sold him a tract of land in the beautiful North Street district of Greenwich adjoining the lovely estate of Mrs. Walter

Pierson, to whom years previously I had sold a tract of land owned by the Albert F. Bowerman estate, on which she had built one of the outstanding country homes in Greenwich. When I showed this property to Mr. Thompson he was very much intrigued, and planned to construct a road from North Street running to the rear of the property which overlooked the beautiful Greenwich Reservoir lake, and named the street Loch Lane. This was a most desirable location for fine country homes, and a number of very attractive residences designed by Mr. Thompson, including his own, were built by him. He was indeed an architect with great skill and exquisite taste combined with energy and initiative.

In the early days of 1929, one of my friends, Mr. Arthur W. Francis, who had built a very attractive estate on the banks of the Mianus River in Stamford, advised me that he wished to sell, and I set our office actively at work on the job. It developed that Mr. Ormsby M. Mitchel, an active Wall Street broker who was very fond of horses and riding, decided to acquire an estate in Connecticut. The Francis property, with its many features and adjoining bridle paths, seemed ideally suited to Mr. Mitchel's requirements, and we succeeded in making the sale.

Mr. Thomas G. Terbell, who had constructed a very attractive colonial house at the corner of Taconic and South Stanwich Road in Greenwich, offered the property for sale and, as I admired the property very much, I made him an offer of purchase. After some negotiation, he accepted. The house was of moderate size but excellently planned, and my wife and I enjoyed it very much as a place of residence. Pictures of it are shown in this book. Several years later, I sold the property to Mr. Harry K. Barr whose wife admired it very much. The Barrs added to and improved the property in many ways, but Mr. Barr finally decided he wished a larger tract of land where he planned to build a house of luxurious type with all the rooms on one floor. We placed his house on the market and sold it to Mr. Burton Cutler, after which we sold Mr. Barr a property with many acres of land, a farm cottage and some farm buildings, on the upper end of Lake Avenue, Greenwich. He built the ideal house that he had dreamed of. The house was indeed a most exceptional one in every way, and he and Mrs. Barr enjoyed it immensely. Unfortunately, Mr. Barr's death brought about a complete change in plans, and the property was sold to Mr. and Mrs. J. S. Hewitt who now occupy it.

Shortly after I sold my house on Taconic Road to Mr. Barr, I

View of the residence on Taconic Road in North Greenwich purchased by Mr. Howe from Thomas G. Terbell.

decided to purchase a residence in the Brookside Park area of Greenwich which was in a most accessible and interesting location. I must say that the house proved a most delightful place of residence, and I occupied it until my wife's death. Then I sold it to Dr. John F. Grady, a well-known New York surgeon, and his wife, who with their most attractive children have occupied the property since then.

One of the pleasantest recollections of my whole real-estate career was the meeting and the many enjoyable visits which I had with Mr. and Mrs. Edward J. Nally. Mr. Nally was one of the organizers and the first president of the Radio Corporation of America. After retiring as president, he chose to live in Greenwich where I sold him an ample house in Belle Haven. He had some very interesting collections, including antiques and historical objects, and enjoyed showing them to his friends. He was a very close friend of David Sarnoff, the present head of R.C.A., and often mentioned their early experiences together. Later, during World War II, I sold his Greenwich home to Viscount Van de Vyvere, a Belgian financier who had managed to escape to America when the Nazis occupied Belgium.

Our office at this time had become very active in the upper end of Westchester County, and one of the sales that stands out in my memory was the sale of the estate of Nola L. Mandell to Otto E. Koegel. Mr. Koegel, a New York lawyer, had a suburban home in Bronxville at the time. Coming from the West, he had a longing for acreage and farms. I showed him the upper areas of Westchester, and they appealed strongly to him. He bought the Mandell estate at Granite Springs, and then bought adjoining properties. He soon found himself drawn into the breeding of first class cattle. He has done a great deal to develop this area of Westchester north of Croton Lake. In fact, he interested one of his law partners in buying an estate nearby, and we sold this partner, Mr. Ralph S. Harris, the Charles F. Tannerhill estate in Somers which included a lake, brook, a lovely farm house, and numerous farm buildings. For many years Mr. Harris

The attractive estate of Mr. E. J. Nally in Greenwich.   The very attractive farm estate of Mr. Samuel H. Golding in Stamford.

operated this estate as a gentleman's farm. Mr. Charles F. Tannerhill also had a lovely place at nearby Lake Mahopac which we sold to Dr. Eugene J. Bozan.

During the depression of 1929, real estate, like all other business, was depressed. The demand for suburban homes and estates was much less than it had been, and the development of the suburban villages and towns seemed to stand still. Many developers were caught in the down surge and lost fortunes. This was especially true where the properties or developments were burdened with large mortgages of short duration. Banks and mortgage companies had gone into the practice of lending very large sums on vacant land and gentlemen's estates, and many of these properties were foreclosed and offered for resale at a fraction of their former values.

After the depression had run its course, it took many years to recover the losses which had been sustained. However, I can say from personal observation that Westchester, with its many charms and advantages, was one of the first suburban areas to recover. As an illustration, in 1932 we sold the very fine estate of Adolph F. Stone in Chappaqua to Mr. Joseph B. Marini, one of New York's leading importers. Also we sold to Mr. Edward Wise, one of the partners in the Wall Street firm of Bache and Company, a wonderful gentleman's estate in Stamford which for many years had been developed by Samuel J. Taylor. Mr. Taylor was the publisher of the popular magazine, *Rider and Driver,* and naturally took great interest in horses. In fact, the elaborate Stamford Horse Show was annually held on his property. He had purchased an original colonial house. With it he acquired many acres of land contiguous to the main residence. Through the property ran the Mianus River which had been dammed up, creating a swimming lake and a waterfall. It was generally considered to be a most distinguished country place. Mr. Wise added to and improved the property in many ways. I have many pleasant memories of interesting visits to the property.

About this same time, Halsey W. Kent, who for many years had owned and operated the famous Kent House in Greenwich, had an interview with me and suggested that he might sell Kent House if he found a suitable buyer. The hotel had a long tradition of first quality. It had grace and a most desirable clientele. It was operated as a summer hotel. Many summer visitors wound up by buying beautiful estates for permanent homes in Greenwich. Jokingly, it was called the cradle of Greenwich.

Mr. Kent was advancing in years and wanted to sell only if the buyer would carry out the fine tradition of the place. Mr. Edward C. Fogg, who had previously managed the Plaza Hotel and the Roosevelt Hotel in New York, was retiring from large hotel operation and discussed with me the possibility of finding a small hotel in the nearby suburbs. The Kent House seemed made to order for his requirements, and I brought about a sale of the property to him. He certainly carried on its best traditions for many years until his death when his widow sold it. It continued on with its high standards until the planners of the New England Thruway came along. This thruway ran directly through the Kent House which was torn down—one of the "tragedies of progress."

Our office kept extending its activities further and further into Connecticut, and I remember that at about this time we sold, in co-operation with local brokers, the country place of Princess Constance Pignatelli in Madison, Connecticut to Alexander Calder. It was situated beyond New Haven on the Sound in Connecticut. The Lois Clarke estate at Stockbridge in the Berkshires in Massachusetts, we sold to John H. Hopkins, and the A. T. Baker property in Old Saybrook to Cecil Lyon.

Early in 1935, a beautiful estate on Dingletown Road in Greenwich, which had previously been the home of Garrett C. Pier, was sold by our office to Baron John Von Leidersdorff and his attractive wife. They proceeded to improve the premises and certainly succeeded in creating an ideal country estate. Change of plans caused them to sell the property, and in the fall of 1935 Mrs. F. B. Hufnagel, whose husband was the president of the Crucible Steel Company, inquired about some properties which we had advertised. I arranged to take her on an inspection trip. When she saw the Von Leidersdorff place she was very much impressed with its many advantages, and arranged to have her husband inspect the property thoroughly with her. Mr. Hufnagel made a most careful study of the property from every point of view and, after some negotiations, he bought it. Even though the property had considerable acreage already, he bought a large tract of adjoining land and improved it greatly. With streams and several private ponds, trees and rare shrubbery, the property stood out as among the most handsome in the Greenwich area.

Huffnagel Estate in Greenwich.

The present Wyman Estate in Greenwich.

CHAPTER XIV

UPPER WESTCHESTER

A VERY INTERESTING SALE was made by Mr. Hyatt to Mr. Donald McConaughy, in Northern Westchester near Brewster. This was a most attractive countryside even though it was somewhat distant from New York from a commuting standpoint. It was, nevertheless, considered a most delightful spot for a country estate. The surrounding country has many hills and lakes. It is high ground, a very healthful, dry and delightful climate. There is a ridge of land running east and west just below the village of Brewster known as Dingle Ridge, and a road known as the Dingle Ridge Road runs along this ridge and passes many very interesting country places. At the very end of Dingle Ridge one of the most delightful of all was the beautiful farm estate of Mr. J. C. Bolger. It contained a colonial country house, many excellent farm buildings, beautiful fields for grazing cattle and every feature to make it a practical farm. Mr. McConaughy considered it the most interesting and desirable property that he had inspected, and after some negotiation Mr. Hyatt made the sale.

I can also report a series of sales of one of the most attractive country estates near Bedford Village in Northern Westchester. Mr. Nicholas Rutgers, an idealist, had purchased acreage near Bedford Village just north of the country club which had a magnificent view of the entire surrounding countryside. He proceeded to build a French Provincial house with an entrance courtyard and all of the attractive features of this type of architecture. The house was large enough for gracious living, had a farm cottage and other farm buildings. There was a stream, pond and every desirable feature that a prospective purchaser desires. Situated as it was, way back from the main road on an entrance roadway, one felt indeed that he was examining a lovely European estate.

Mr. Rutgers finally decided to sell the property, and I inspected it and was very much entranced. We showed it to many of our clients, but because of the size and luxurious accommodations it was hard to find just the right purchaser. However, Mr. Hyatt had a Mr. Franklin B. Pollock to whom he had previously rented a country estate, and when he showed the Rutgers property to Mr. and Mrs. Pollock they were very much attracted to it, and eventually purchased it. Mr. Pollock proceeded to add to and beautify the place even more. Several years later, Mr. Pollock's business was transferred to the northern New York area, and it was necessary for him to make a sale. It was so attractive that we promptly sold it to Mr. Benjamin Abrams who lived in it for several years. Later still, we showed it to one of our clients, Mr. P. C. Cartier, a relation of the jewelry family, who had come from France. He was so intrigued with the property that he made an offer and purchased it on his first visit. He certainly enjoyed the place, but as it happens, when the war was over and he could move back to France he decided to do so, and we again had this lovely property for sale. Without much effort we succeeded in finding a buyer, a Mr. William C. Loehmann. The picture of the house tells its own story.

In the early part of 1933, our office made a very interesting sale of a property in Katonah consisting of approximately forty acres of land on a ridge near the village and commanding long-distance views. The residence was the property of the Joseph F. Dowd estate which was sold by our office to Mr. and Mrs. Julius Brandenburg who at that time were residing in lower Westchester. They were fond of riding and wished to be where they could have horses and country life. They certainly made a most interesting and attractive development of this estate.

In the summer of 1934, we made a sale in Ardsley Park, Ardsley-on-the-Hudson, which attracted considerable attention. It was the sale of the outstanding estate of Mrs. Justine B. Ward, in co-operation with the William B. May Company, to Frank Gould. The Goulds had always been drawn to this area along the Hudson River. Edwin Gould had a magnificent estate on the Hudson at Ardsley, his mother-in-law had an estate in Ardsley Park, his sister Helen (Mrs. Finley Sheppard), had a large estate a little further north near Tarrytown, so it seemed natural for Frank Gould to choose Ardsley Park. This he did, and when he died he left it to the New York University for college purposes, a fine and generous act.

Another sale we made was that of the lovely estate of F. Julius Fohs situated on King Street, Chappaqua, to Philip Haberman. The property adjoined one of the lakes on the large Guinzburg Estate. The residence was situated on a hill far in from the road. It was indeed a picture.

Properties even as far out as Carmel became popular, and one

The Brandenberg Estate in Katonah, New York.

The Pollock Estate sold to Mr. Loehmann in Bedford, New York.

of our sales in this area was the estate of Sarah Parks Reed to John S. Burke, president of B. Altman and Company of New York.

We made a sale in which I took a special interest because of the esteem which I had for its late owner. It was the estate of Herman Metz, who prior to his death had been one of New York's really great men of his day. He was not only a very much respected and successful business man, but gave a great part of his time and ability to public service. The Metz estate, which was situated on a site on the shore of Long Island Sound at Orienta Point, Mamaroneck, was sold by my office to a New York business man, Arthur T. Levine.

CHAPTER XV

IN THE HILLS OF GREENWICH AND STAMFORD

THE READER WILL RECALL that I have mentioned the sale of one of the houses on the palatial Converse estate in Greenwich to Mr. Knickerbocker and then to Mr. Platt. In 1935, the Bankers Trust Company of New York listed with us for sale the main Converse estate. It was such a large and valuable property that I realized that it could only be sold to a man of great means for his residence, or to a wealthy developer for subdivision. One day I received a telephone call from Mrs. Lewis Rosenstiel whose husband is the head of the Schenley Distillers Company, saying that I had been recommended to her by one of our clients. She was interested in purchasing a house with charm and a fairly large piece of land not too far from New York City, and preferably with a lake on it, as her husband loved to fish. I arranged trips of inspection with Mrs. Rosenstiel, but no property then available appealed to her, and particularly Mr. Rosenstiel kept

Long distance view of magnificent main residence on Converse Estate.

View of Converse Lake on Converse Estate.

insisting on a lake. I kept going over our listings, but the only one which remotely covered her requirements was the Converse estate in Greenwich with its wonderful lake, but I hardly dared to show it, feeling that its cost would be prohibitive. Finally, I mustered up enough courage to make an appointment to show the property to Mr. and Mrs. Rosenstiel without mentioning price. When it came time to show the lake, I took them to the lakehouse. The water was as clear as crystal and the scene indeed entrancing. The main residence seemed too large, but the smaller residence with a few changes and redecoration might serve their requirements. Mr. Rosenstiel was enthusiastic about the lake, but the tremendous size of the acreage, apple orchards, many farm buildings, and elaborate equipment, and the total cost posed a problem. He mentioned that perhaps he might consider it as a real estate investment. Shortly after that, he made a trip to Europe. I hardly dreamed it possible that he might buy it, but to my surprise and delight when he returned from Europe the head of the real-estate division of the Bankers Trust Company rang me up one day and said that Mr. Rosenstiel, who was one of their leading patrons, would like him to call with me at his apartment in New York to discuss the Converse estate. After a brief interview, during which the bank official named the minimum cash price that the bank would consider, he decided to buy it. And thus the Converse estate became the property of Lewis S. Rosenstiel individually and as trustee, to which he still holds title. Mr. Rosenstiel later acquired many additional neighboring acres of land. The estate is ideally situated for eventual development into a residential section of note which will continue its fame for all time.

Before I leave my recollections of Greenwich and the Converse estate, I might add that a residence on the estate, with approximately fourteen acres of land, which I had originally sold to Mr. Knickerbocker and later resold to Mr. Platt, later still I sold to Max Horowitz, a New York financier. Finally, it again came on the market and was sold by me to Mr. James O. McCue, the head of the Stamford Rolling Mills, one of Stamford's leading industries. Mr. and Mrs. McCue remodeled the house with exquisite taste, built a swimming pool with artistic pavilion, beautified the land with lovely gardens, lawns and rare shrubbery so that today this house is a gem of the first quality.

Theodore Blake, the New York architect, lived in an attractive country residence at the junction of Lafayette Avenue and the Boston Post Road in Greenwich. He was a close friend of some of my best friends, and I had the pleasure of seeing him often. He and his family controlled a considerable land frontage on the Boston Post Road opposite the Pickwick Arms Hotel, one of the most desirable tracts zoned for business in Greenwich. He decided to place the property on the market. We succeeded, in co-operation with the firm of Banks and Cleveland in Greenwich, in selling the corner plot to the First National Bank of Greenwich which was looking for a site for their own building including all the advantages of an office building as well. The Bank, now The Fairfield County Trust Company, is an outstanding one, and its location is an exceptionally desirable one for its depositors. The adjoining frontage on the Boston Post Road has now been developed with attractive stores.

The land back of the Blake property, situated on Church Street which was zoned permitting the construction of an apartment house, was sold by our office to Mr. Alfred Kaskel, the New York builder, who constructed on it an apartment house of the highest quality called Town and Country apartments. Shortly after this pleasant introduction to Mr. Kaskel I interested him in purchasing a country estate in Connecticut. After showing him many properties with large acreage and attractive residences, I interested him, in co-operation with Blakeman Quintard Meyer, in the home of Mr. and Mrs. T. M. Godde in Stamford on Roxbury Road. Mrs. Godde was the daughter of Mr. Dodge of automobile fame, and after her death her husband

The beautiful estate of J. C. McCue in Greenwich, which was part of the original Converse Estate.

The beautiful Spiekerman Estate in Greenwich sold to Mr. George W. Fennell.

desired to sell their very attractive home. Mr. Kaskel, with his keen understanding of real estate and its merits, could see its possibilities and made the purchase. I later sold him adjoining acreage, and his property today is one of the finest in the nearby Connecticut countryside.

At about this same time, we sold a house in Greenwich with a genuine colonial history and tradition in its record. It had been part of the Field estate which had been sold to the actress, Ina Claire. Miss Claire, with great skill, had modernized the house but retained its great beauty of design and construction. When she decided to move to the West she placed the property on the market. Located as it was in the northern section of Greenwich near the Round Hill district and Yale Farms, it appealed to the exacting buyer. We sold it to Mr. and Mrs. Edward L. Blackman who for many years kept adding to the beauty and attractiveness of the house and grounds. Later when the property again came on the market, Mr. Terrell Van Ingen of our office sold it to Mr. and Mrs. Donald Duncan.

For a number of years, Mr. Atherton W. Hobler, one of the heads of the advertising firm of Benton and Bowles, Inc., had been interested in breeding cattle. He had an estate situated on Newfield Avenue in Stamford, with beautiful fields, a lovely colonial house and excellent farm buildings, but as time went on he desired larger acreage and authorized me to place his house for sale. At about this

The fine office building constructed by the First National Bank of Greenwich on the Blake Estate on the Post Road in Greenwich.

Business buildings on the Post Road, Greenwich, on the balance of the Post Road frontage of the Blake Estate.

time I became acquainted with Samuel H. Golding, banker and New York real-estate operator, and Mr. Golding and his wife desired to acquire a country place in the nearby Connecticut area. I made many trips of inspection with them, and finally they decided that Mr. Hobler's estate would serve their requirements. After some negotiation I made the sale to Mr. Golding, who proceeded to enlarge and beautify the property, built a swimming pool, and added outdoor cooking and dining facilities. He also enlarged and improved the barns and decided to develop one of the finest herds of Guernsey cattle in the country. He indeed has a wonderful estate.

In 1934, I made a sale to George Walden, an executive of the Standard Vacuum Oil Company who later became its president. Mr. Walden purchased through us a country property north of Greenwich adjoining the estate of Sterling Rockefeller on East Middle Patent Road belonging to the Oboschelle Corporation. He later purchased a large tract of land nearby, intending to build a new residence thereon, but the death of his wife changed his plans, and I sold his house to Col. William L. Brookfield, and the nearby acreage to Norman Spelke who developed it into an attractive residential district.

Before World War II, the country had not fully recovered from the 1929 depression, but still progress continued in suburban development. The building of the parkways and the many improvements

The beautiful estate of Mr. Alfred Kaskel in Stamford.

Estate of Mr. Mortimer H. Hess in Stamfor

The main residence on the extensive Cooper Estate in Stamford.

The private lake on the Cooper Estate.

which were added to suburban facilities drew increasing numbers of new residents from the city. Real-estate taxes were low and income taxes were much less than they are today. The struggle for advancement was well under way, and property values which had suffered so severely during the depression were gradually improving. To one riding through the suburbs on good roads in a modern automobile, progress was evident on all sides. New public schools, new town buildings and improved parks added to the picture, and everyone was confident of rapid advancement. This state of mind greatly helped us in making sales of suburban real estate.

Mr. and Mrs. Sherman Hoyt had developed a very lovely country estate on the north side of Cross River Reservoir near Katonah in Northern Westchester. Mrs. Hoyt took a great interest in breeding dogs and had constructed model dog kennels on her property, which became famous among dog lovers. It was indeed a beautiful place. However, as time went on, her mother built a magnificent home between Greenwich and Stamford in north Greenwich, and Mrs. Hoyt desired to move into that area. We listed her property for sale, and Mr. Hyatt of our office succeeded in selling it to Mr. Albert Turner, one of our special clients. Mr. Turner proceeded to add to and glorify the property which today is one of the outstanding estates in this area.

Mrs. Sherman Hoyt and her husband eventually moved to Long Ridge Road in Stamford, where she transferred her kennels. The pictures show the house after it had been added to and modified by her and her husband. Several years ago, they decided to sell. Mr. Terrell Van Ingen had a client of ours, Mr. Richard Salomon, who had a lovely place in Stamford but desired a larger home. After some negotiation he sold the Hoyt place to him.

At about this same time, we sold the beautiful Wykoff estate on West Mountain Road in Ridgefield to the New York art dealer, Mr. Felix Wildenstein. We sold it in co-operation with Luther Brown, one of our allied brokers, who specialized in the Westport, Wilton and Ridgefield areas and with whom we had many very pleasant relations.

In 1937, about two years before World War II started, I had a call one day from Dr. Charles V. Paterno who was one of New York's greatest builders. He had built many of New York's fine apartment houses, including 270 Park Avenue. He had built a castle for his own occupancy on Washington Heights overlooking the Hudson River. There he had one of the finest greenhouses in the country, where the most beautiful orchids were grown. As mentioned, his love of the country and horticulture had drawn him to a district in Westchester near Armonk where he developed the Windmill Farm, He developed a magnificent horticultural garden. He was a man with great imagination, extraordinary energy, and intelligence. These qualities carried him to great achievements. He never gave up when he started out to accomplish something.

Residence of Mr. and Mrs. Sherman Hoyt in Stamford.

View of the former Dalsemer Estate in Greenwich.

One day, it occurred to him that he would like a piece of land in Greenwich near Windmill Farm. I took him around and was amazed that, even though he was partly crippled as a result of a fall from a horse some years before, he managed to climb over stone walls and up hills in examining various undeveloped sites. While looking around, he saw in the distance a hilltop in north Greenwich and suggested that we look at it. It was the famous Round Hill, the highest spot along the Sound between New York and Boston. It was always greatly admired in Greenwich, and gave its name to the residential area around it, the Round Hill District. I told Dr. Paterno that none of Round Hill was for sale. He kept talking about it and refused to look at anything else. I finally agreed to take him for a walk up to the top of the hill along an old footpath. When we reached the top and walked around we saw magnificent views in all directions. He looked and looked and finally told me that this was the location that he wanted me to buy for him to build a home. The property was owned by a New York lawyer, William L. Cummings, who had an estate next door where he lived. He had bought Round Hill some years previously just to keep it from being built upon, and of course he did not want to sell.

Dr. Paterno kept after me as months went by, and I repeated my efforts with Mr. Cummings but without success. Finally, I was told by an expert that Round Hill would not be suitable for a residence because no trees would grow on it, due to the fact that the top soil was only four feet deep and below this was hardpan so that ground water would not drain away. Therefore if one dug a hole it would fill with water and not drain off. The result was that trees with roots died because the roots decayed. When I heard this explanation of why there were no trees on Round Hill, knowing how much Dr. Paterno loved trees and would want them if he built a house, I thought my problem was solved. When I told this to Dr. Paterno I thought that he would give up the idea of Round Hill and let me show him some other property, but his reaction was exactly the opposite. "Who said I could not grow trees on Round Hill?" was his question. "Just get the property for me and see what I will do." I gave up. The task seemed hopeless.

Later on, general business conditions were not so bright, and I happened to meet Mr. Cummings on the train to New York one morning and told him again that he ought to let me sell part of Round Hill to Dr. Paterno who would build a house that would be a credit to the neighborhood and would certainly not hurt the view from his place. Later still, I had another talk with him, and he finally said that he would sell about twenty-three acres of it with certain restrictions, but his minimum price would be $6,000 per acre. This indeed sounded high, and knowing how careful and shrewd a buyer Dr. Paterno was, I thought this would finally take his mind off the demand for Round Hill. But when I told him, all he said was, "Well, I'll take it, draw up the contract." When I reported this back to Mr. Cummings he was stumped. He really did not want to sell and hardly knew what to say. But he was a man who kept his word. A contract was signed by both parties, and Dr. Paterno became the owner of Round Hill. When I reminded him about what I had told him about trees not growing on Round Hill, he just laughed and said, "Watch me." The first thing he did was to dig many deep trenches, deeper than the hardpan, from the top of Round Hill down to the bottom, close together all around the hill. Then he dug circular trenches, circling the hill close together, also from the top to the bottom. He placed drains and water pipes in the trenches. There were valves to turn water on the roots of trees if they needed it. The drains took away surplus water. The result was that he transplanted to and grew on Round Hill the finest group of trees to be found anywhere, including a famous old tree of great size that stood before the church on Riversville Road, corner of John Street near Round Hill, which he bought. The transporting and re-planting of it, was a job of great difficulty and great cost. Has anyone ever met a man who carried out his determined purpose more completely? When he finally built his house on Round Hill, one of his real pleasures was to take me around and show me how he had grown a very great many trees when it had been considered impossible.

Famous Paterno residence on the top of Round Hill, Greenwich.

The estate of Henry H. Reichhold in the Whippoorwill Country Club area, Chappaqua.

CHAPTER XVI

CENTRAL WESTCHESTER AND CONNECTICUT

ONE OF THE PLEASANTEST RECOLLECTIONS of my real-estate career was the sale of the beautiful Christiancy estate, situated on the south side of Ridge Road, west of Central Avenue near Hartsdale opposite the large park area of the Sprain Brook Park System. The property had always appealed to me. It included a large acreage and a charming residence situated on a beautiful entrance road well back from the main highway. Being on a hill, it commanded long-distance views. Beautiful woods, a stream and brook, fields and outbuildings complete the picture. A New York manufacturer and business leader, Henry J. Gaisman, had inquired about suburban estates, and I personally agreed to meet him and show him what was available. This proved to be one of the most delightful tasks that I had ever undertaken. Mr. Gaisman was a widely read and most interesting personality. We inspected various properties, including the Christiancy estate which appealed to him. He offered to lease the estate with the

Estate of Henry J. Gaisman in Hartsdale.

The Campagna Estate in Riverdale.   The beautiful O'Brien Estate in Park Hill, Yonkers.

privilege of purchase if he found after trial that it covered his requirements. The owner accepted these terms. After a few months of trial,
Mr. Gaisman purchased the property and also a number of additional parcels of land contiguous to it, winding up with more than
125 acres of land. He modified and improved the house so that it
became one of the most elegant homes to be found anywhere. The
grounds and the roads through the fields and the woods were also
beautiful, and he greatly improved them. Mr. Gaisman took great
personal interest in developing the property, and many a delightful
visit I had with him. We became intimate friends and have remained
so until this day.

Again, one of our most interesting and pleasant memories was the
sale of the estate in Scarsdale owned by E. Gerli and Company, Inc.,
which we had sold to other owners in the past. We were fortunate
in having as a client the diamond expert and jeweler, Harry Winston,
the owner of the Hope Diamond. Mrs. Winston and her husband had
very exacting requirements, and after a most thorough inspection of
properties they selected the property which Mr. Gerli owned. It was
indeed an interesting place, a colonial house of distinction, situated
well back from the highway, surrounded by beautiful grounds and
magnificent trees. There were several cottages and stables, and every
desirable feature of a farm estate, including approximately twenty-four
acres of land.

One of the real estate transactions which passed through my office in 1938, was particularly interesting as it involved individuals who were well known and in the public eye. It seemed that Mr. Edgar Rickard, a close friend of President Hoover, had a lovely estate in New Canaan where President and Mrs. Hoover had visited from time to time so that it stood out in the limelight. I knew him personally, and he told me that he wished to sell. It happened that we had recently listed for sale the country home, in Stamford, of Mignon Eberhart, the mystery writer, who desired a larger house, preferably in New Canaan. I showed her the Rickard house which she was willing to buy if she could sell hers. The thought occurred to me that perhaps I could arrange to have Mr. Rickard take her house in Stamford in part payment, as it was smaller than his and could probably be sold more promptly. After some negotiation I brought about a trade, and shortly thereafter we sold the Stamford house to J. Macey Willets.

With the spirit of trading in our system, we shortly thereafter made a trade of the outstanding estate of Park Rowley, the New York banker, which overlooked Lake Mamanasco in Ridgefield, Connecticut, for the residence of B. E. Levy, the head of the cosmetic firm known as Charles of the Ritz, whose residence was situated in Larchmont Manor. Later we sold the Levy house in Larchmont for Park Rowley to Sidney A. Olson.

Mr. Levy and his wife had lived in France, and they preferred the country to the city. Originally they intended to use the Ridgefield house as a summer place, but both finally decided to make it their year-round home. On its site looking out over Lake Mamanasco, at one of the highest altitudes near New York, it had a delightful and healthful climate all the year round. Mr. and Mrs. Levy loved the estate and proceeded to make extensive additions to it including a dock and beach house on Lake Mamanasco on which the property had a frontage. They lived there until their deaths.

The original owner of this property at Lake Mamanasco in Ridgefield was Mrs. Antoinette R. Peterson. Mrs. Peterson had gone further north in Connecticut after selling her home in Ridgefield and had purchased an estate located in Brookfield Center containing a large amount of acreage and a lovely colonial house and numerous outbuildings. She later decided to sell the property, and got in touch with our office. We had a client, Mr. Remington Korper, who lived on Staten Island and who was interested in the production of plays in the New York theaters. He wanted to find a place well out in the

Main residence in the B. E. Levy Estate overlooking Lake Mamanasco, Ridgefield.

View of Lake Mamanasco from the Levy Estate.

country for himself and his family where he could spend a considerable portion of his time in delightful privacy. I showed him a number of properties in the area north of Ridgefield. He became very much attached to Mrs. Peterson's estate at Brookfield Center, and we succeeded in making a sale to him. He and his family have been enthusiastic residents of the area ever since.

At about this time Mr. A. Rhett du Pont and his wife, were living in Greenwich and desired to purchase a colonial residence with some acreage not too far from the village. This was a difficult thing to find. It happened, however, that Mr. A. S. Blagden had a residence on Lake Avenue adjoining the estate of Percy Rockefeller which enjoyed excellent privacy surrounded by a number of acres of lovely grounds. Mr. and Mrs. du Pont became very much interested in it, and I finally arranged a sale of the property to them.

In the fall of 1945, we were offering a very attractive property situated on a waterfront site in Riverside, Connecticut, owned by Mr. Andrew Kakayannis, who had placed the property on the market. One of our clients at this time was Mr. and Mrs. Irvin J. Brod who were very much interested in a waterfront estate where they could arrange to have a boat come up to their dock and take Mr. Brod to City Island, where he had extensive interests in the boat building industry. The property was ideally suited for his purpose. On it there was a very fine English stone residence splendidly constructed, and he promptly decided to purchase it.

At about this time, we were quite active in Northern Westchester, and succeeded in making sale of the Swain estate situated on the Bedford Center Road, Bedford Hills, to Mr. Sherman M. Bijur. This property included a large tract of land with a colonial house and numerous outbuildings, and is often pointed out by us now as one of the most attractive residences of the neighborhood.

In this same general area on Route 22 near Bedford Village, Rex Cole, who was widely known as the representative of the products of the General Electric Company with many branch offices, had a lovely country residence. He had made a great reputation as a promoter and was very much liked. He had purchased this country house near Bedford to use as his country home. He also had an apartment in New York City. The property contained many acres of land, a most attractive up-to-date home of charm, and several outbuildings. Mr. Archibald R. Graustein had been introduced to me. He, among his many interests, had had a large interest in the paper industry and had taken extensive trips in the forests of Maine where he loved to roam. He wanted a property that had a home of modest size yet had everything that would satisfy his woodland tastes. The Rex Cole property seemed to be ideal for his requirements. I took him and Mrs. Graustein on several inspection trips, and he decided to purchase the property. He has remained there ever since, and in the meanwhile I sold him considerable additional acreage. He built a large swimming pool and other additions so that his estate today is also one of the most attractive in Westchester County.

In June of 1945, we were making a strenuous effort to find a buyer for the estate of Ralph Matthiessen situated near the waterfront in the village of Irvington, a famous district as it was the home of Washington Irving. Mr. Matthiessen and his brother both had large estates, and the one which we were offering for sale was situated in a very desirable location, being close to the village and the railroad station. It appealed to one of our clients, the Seaboard Surety Company, as an excellent location for an office building. The company decided to purchase the property if it could be zoned for such use. After a very extensive effort on the part of our Mr. Russell who had made the sale to the Seaboard Surety Company, we finally helped to obtain a consent from the zoning board for the use of the Matthiessen estate as an office for the Seaboard Surety Company, and the sale

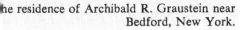
he residence of Archibald R. Graustein near Bedford, New York.

Main residence on the Goodrich Estate.

was consummated. It developed later that other problems arose which decided the Seaboard Surety Company to remain in New York City, and the property was again placed on the market and sold for residential use.

The Russian Revolution which followed World War I caused the notables and the aristocrats of Russia to be eliminated, although many of them were fortunate enough to escape from the country. One of them was Count Lascelle Meserv de Basily who had escaped to France. A short time later, he and his wife came to America intending to make their residence in or near New York City. They had very exacting requirements, and the count had excellent judgment and the highest standards in architecture and design. Not finding his ideal house for sale, I succeeded in selling them a beautiful site in the northern part of Greenwich in the Yale Farms district which enjoyed a magnificent view, had a stream running through the property which could be made into a lake, and many other advantages. The count proceeded to build an ideal type residence of French design. It was in a class by itself, and everyone who saw it praised it highly. As time went on, the count and his wife decided to make their residence in South America, and authorized me to find a purchaser for the property. It was of such exquisite French design that I offered it for sale to Mr. John Frederick Harjes whose father had been one of the partners of Mr. J. P. Morgan in the Paris office. It was natural for Mr. Harjes and his family to become very much interested, and I made the sale. They proceeded to make additions which were greatly admired.

One of the sales made at about this time interested me very much as I was a great admirer of the property which was situated near Ridgefield, Connecticut. It was the home of Mr. James M. Doubleday, and was in an ideal location on West Lane a short distance south of the village of Ridgefield. Mr. Doubleday, who had another home in Ridgefield, decided to sell this estate on West Lane and listed it with our office. About this time, Mr. Robert J. Hoffman, a vicepresident of the Union Carbide and Carbon Company of New York, had inquired about country homes in the Connecticut area. I had Mr. Van Ingen show him many properties, but especially recommended the Doubleday house. Mr. Hoffman, after careful consideration, finally purchased the property and has lived in it ever since. It is one of the gems in its environment.

The country area in the northern section of Stamford, Connecti-

Residence on the estate of Count de Basily in Greenwich.

Main residence on the M. T. Stark Estate in Greenwich.

cut, was always considered one of the very best locations for country homes. The high ground and transportation facilities, including the Hutchinson River Parkway, appealed to businessmen as an excellent location for year-round homes. Mr. Lawrence W. Lowman was one of these, and he had a colonial home on a hill location far back from the highway near the Long Ridge area of Stamford. He and his wife had decorated the house with exquisite taste. We had a client, George A. Stern, who had an estate at Irvington-on-Hudson who decided to move into the hill country back of Stamford. Mr. Stern and his wife had made frequent trips of inspection with me personally of many country places, but nothing available had attracted them. However, when the Lowman house became available, it proved to be exactly their dream house, and even though they had a home in Irvington which had not yet been sold, I managed to sell the property to them. I promptly got on the job and sold their Irvington home to Mrs. Elizabeth Walsh Long in co-operation with the New York office of one of our associated brokers, William B. May and Company.

CHAPTER XVII

GREENWICH AND WHIPPOORWILL

AMONG THE INTERESTING TASKS that I had as a real-estate broker was a sale of land which I made to Mr. R. M. Hillas, who was the head of the Columbia Carbon Company, and who, with his wife, wanted an ideal site on the water front in Greenwich where they could build the perfect house. Mr. Hillas had engineering skill and could design a house with exceptionally good taste and judgment. I showed him many water front sites, and at one time I thought that I might be able to sell him a large part of the tip end of Mead's Point. We kept looking. Finally he and his wife were attracted to the water front known as Benedict's Point. There was a parcel of land at the end of Benedict's Point which the estate had authorized us to offer for sale. Mr. and Mrs. Hillas selected a site which on one side had a sheltered water front. The front faced out over Long Island Sound. Mr. Hillas designed a most attractive colonial house, and when it was finished he had a great party including all those who had something to do with the construction of the residence, and I must say it was

Main residence on the Ladas Estate at Riverside, Greenwich.

a wonderful event. The house stands out as a masterpiece of architecture.

One of the important business leaders of his time was Mr. W. R. Addicks, who was the head of the Consolidated Gas Company of New York. He had built a most interesting and attractive farm estate in the Westchester Hills near Mt. Kisco. Included with the 143 acres

Residence on the estate of the late Mr. R. M. Hillas
on Benedict Point, Greenwich.

of land was an artistic colonial house, farm buildings, and fields for the cattle grazing. As time went on, Mr. Addicks decided to move to Greenwich, Connecticut, where he acquired an estate on North Maple Avenue. Mr. Addicks got in touch with me and listed the property in Mount Kisco for sale, but we were not successful in finding a satisfactory buyer. A short time later, Mr. Addicks died which was a great shock to all who knew him. Lawyers representing his estate requested us to make a sale of both the properties. We found a purchaser for the Mount Kisco property, which has since been developed into a most attractive suburban residential park. The property in Greenwich did not sell rapidly, and I was instructed by the counsel representing the estate to offer the property for sale at auction which was a job that I had seldom undertaken. However, at this auction sale in Greenwich, the property was sold to a Catholic order which used it for many years, finally disposing of it to the Greenwich Academy.

In 1946, Mr. John McHugh, who had built a country estate in the Whippoorwill Country Club area near Chappaqua, requested that I visit his house and discuss its possible sale. I had always admired the property and must say that when I made a thorough inspection of the house, it was the most luxurious and expensively constructed residence that I had ever seen. Mr. McHugh had spent a fortune in building the property. The market for property of this type was not very active, and we did not succeed in finding any buyer for several

Main residence on the Addicks Estate.

years, even though Mr. McHugh was in constant touch with us. He died several years later, and his widow requested me to put forth a special effort to sell, as the house was entirely too large for her needs. Finally, we were advised that Mr. Henry H. Reichhold of the Reichhold Chemical Company was planning to move from Detroit to New York, and we arranged for him and his wife to inspect properties in the hills of Westchester. After a complete search of available properties, Mr. Reichhold advised me that the McHugh property suited their requirements if the price were satisfactory. We were fortunate in being able to arrange terms of purchase which were satisfactory to both parties, and Mr. and Mrs. Reichhold moved into the McHugh estate. They have improved it beyond description, and it certainly takes first rank among the fine estates in its neighborhood.

Ritchie Estate in Somers.   Loeb Estate in Mount Kisco.

Addicks Estate in Greenwich.   Mitchel Estate in Stamford.

Publicity is a great assistance to the real-estate agent, especially if it is good publicity, and any purchases through an agent to a very important person is a bit of news that is widely publicized. Walter Winchell and his wife desired to purchase a country place in the nearby Westchester suburbs. We were fortunate in being the brokers who were selected to find a property for him, and Mr. Russell of my office, with a great deal of skill, managed to find a suitable property on the Fort Hill Road in the Scarsdale area. We succeeded in selling it to Mr. Winchell and avoided publicity even though we would have benefited by it. This certainly required exceptional skill, and we often commended Mr. Russell for his tact in this case.

Another case in which we avoided extensive publicity was the sale of a property in the hills back of Greenwich to Morton Downey, the singer. Mr. Downey had been extensively looking through the country with our office, and finally decided he would like to live in the area north of Greenwich, but he wanted a very high and sightly location. He wound up selecting a farm on the Stanwich Road of considerable acreage with long-distance views. There was an early American farm house on the property and a very large barn quite a distance in from the street. He promptly tore down the farm house and started to alter the very large barn. He wound up building an elaborate house with many tremendous rooms. He certainly made it a most interesting and attractive estate. After a number of years, he decided to sell the property. We succeeded in finding a buyer in Mr. Harry E. Gould who purchased additional land and beautified the estate greatly. Among the most interesting new features was a very large swimming pool with a cabaña and other lovely facilities.

Main residence and attractive entrance road on the Harry E. Gould, formerly Morton Downey, Estate in Greenwich.

CHAPTER XVIII

AFTER WORLD WAR II

WORLD WAR II which started in 1939 in Europe depressed the real-estate market which had been gradually recovering after the 1929 depression. Estates, like the beautiful home of Maurice Brill in Mount Kisco, were sold by our office at a substantial discount. However, with persistence and energy we succeeded in making a certain number of sales, only to be shocked two years later by the Japanese attack at Pearl Harbor which drew us into the war. All our resources were needed for victory which finally came in August, 1945. During this period, development in the suburban area quieted down. Many town and village improvements were postponed and new building came almost to a halt. Notwithstanding all of this, we succeeded in selling the estate in Stamford of Kathryn Gerdau to Mr. Leon Lauterstein, the New York lawyer. He and his wife, with exceptional judgment and good taste, have made this among the most attractive country homes in Stamford.

In this period, we also sold the Budlong residence in Greenwich to Harold W. Comfort, now the president of the Borden Company. Another sale was the Logan Estate on Lake Mamanasco in Ridgefield to Mrs. Victoria Tenger.

Another outstanding sale of this period was that of the water front estate of R. A. Stranahan at Westport, to Candler Dobbs. This brick colonial house on a high knoll overlooking the Long Island Sound was one of the largest water front estates on the Sound within commuting distance of New York. When Mr. Stranahan, the industrialist, advised me that he wished to sell, I searched our records until I came to the name of Candler Dobbs, who then lived in Greenwich but wanted a water front property farther out in the country. When he inspected the Stranahan property, it appealed to him strongly, and I arranged the sale with Mr. Stranahan who was then in Florida.

It is often very difficult to find just the right property for a client who has very definite requirements, and I remember a sale which we made to Mr. Walter W. Friend, counsel for the Metropolitan Life Insurance Company, that solved such a problem perfectly. We had been showing Mr. and Mrs. Friend many country houses, but none

Main residence of the former Tenger Estate on Lake Mamanasco, Ridgefield, Connecticut.

seemed to interest them until I had them inspect the property of Mrs. W. F. Decker on Zaccheus Mead Lane in Greenwich. It was a stone residence on a hill, far in from the road, ample but not too big, overlooking a private lake, on the borderline of the property which had been created by damming an active brook. Fishing, swimming, and boating could be enjoyed. All this was in the most desirable and easily accessible district of North Rock Ridge, Greenwich. I promptly made a sale of the property to Mr. and Mrs. Friend, who certainly have made it one of the handsomest' homes in Greenwich.

About this time, one of our customers was Morton Bronson, an official of the Texas Oil Company, who was renting a home in Greenwich. We finally showed him an estate on Clapboard Ridge Road, Greenwich, opposite Khakum Wood, which had the elegance and grace characteristic of many mansions of Georgian design. The estate belonged to Mr. Gordon Grand who had moved away to northwest Connecticut and desired to sell promptly. Mr. Bronson bought it, and he and his family have enjoyed it ever since.

A sale which reflected the strong appeal of Greenwich as an ideal homeplace to the most exacting and experienced real-estate minds, was the sale of the estate of Mrs. Sonia Orloff on Sherwood Avenue, to the late Mr. Moses Ginsberg, who was one of New York's most

Former Dominick Estate in Stamford.

Former Reed Estate in New Canaan.   Walter W. Friend Estate in Greenwich.

successful builders. He was also very successful in the shipping business as well. He was a man whose good judgment and taste were to
be highly valued. After careful search, he selected and bought the
property of Mrs. Orloff situated on the Byram River in Riversville,
Greenwich, which had been dammed up, making a beautiful private
lake as part of the estate. The main house was of English architecture
on a high site of considerable acreage, including farm buildings for

farming if desired. Mr. Ginsberg bought the property and improved it greatly, building two additional houses for members of his family. Excellent tennis courts, a large swimming pool, new entrance driveways, beautiful landscaping and planting illustrate the skill, the imagination and excellent taste of the owner.

he famous Blake Estate, Greenwich, sold to Mr. Frank Hosford.

The Moses Ginsberg Estate in Greenwich.

Samuel H. Golding Estate in Stamford.

Dolce Building in Chappaqua.

At about this time, we made a very interesting sale of the estate of Dr. Horace H. Holt. It was situated in the Zaccheus Mead Lane district, Greenwich, on a beautiful hill site which was widely admired. Two sisters, Mercedes and Carmen de Arengo, were the buyers.

Also in the neighboring Stanwich Road area we were offering for sale the estate of Ludsford P. Yandell which was one of the outstanding estates of the area and which we sold to Mr. Ernest G. Brown.

We sold an estate on Sherwood Avenue in the Riversville Road district of Greenwich, owned and developed by Mrs. Georgine Boomer. The house was very unusual and attractive. It originally had been built by the artist Hobart Ford. In many respects, it copied the plan of an English castle. It was of stone construction with a central castle-type entrance, a large living room and a very elaborate first floor plan with a large terrace overlooking a private lake which Mrs. Boomer had created by damming an active stream which ran through the property. We sold the property to Dr. J. Albert Avrack, an official of the United States Life Insurance Company, and many additions and improvements were added to the estate during the following years. Finally, Dr. Avrack offered the property for sale, and it was sold by us to Mrs. Patricia W. Teran who also added much to the charm of the property.

As a sequel to the sale of Mrs. Boomer's property in Greenwich to Dr. Avrack, we found that she was interested in purchasing an unusually attractive property on the shore of Long Island Sound in an ideal location. Such a property came on the market after the death of Mr. L. D. Armstrong, who had built an ideal home of which he was very proud, in the Riverside section of Greenwich. We brought about a sale of the property to Mrs. Boomer, who with her exquisite taste proceeded to glorify the property to such an extent that it was irresistible. Later on in the year, Mrs. Boomer advised me that she would be willing to sell the house, and I showed it to the family of one of our clients, Mr. Stephen P. Ladas, a New York lawyer. He and his family were greatly attracted by the merits of the property. After some negotiation we made a sale to Mr. Ladas.

In 1950, we were offering for sale a very interesting farm estate situated on Newfield Avenue, Stamford, just north of the Hutchinson River Parkway. The property had beautiful fields, a colonial residence and miscellaneous farm buildings. One of our clients, Mr. Mortimer H. Hess, who had been referred to me by friends and in whom I took

The Boomer Estate in Greenwich, sold to Mrs. Teran.

special interest, made an extensive search for a property in the neighboring suburbs, which would have the feeling of country life at its best. This property on Newfield Avenue appealed strongly to him and he bought it. Promptly thereafter, Mr. Hess developed some of the land on the west side of Newfield Avenue opposite the main house, and it is today a most interesting estate.

In the upper North Street district of Greenwich, opposite the famous Converse estate, there was a ridge commanding long-distance views of the surrounding area way out to Long Island Sound, and far into the hills of Connecticut. Mr. Frank Spiekerman, who was one of the heads of the Burroughs Adding Machine Company during his lifetime, had built a country home at the end of a long road leading into North Street. His wife, Mrs. Spiekerman, was a very close friend of my wife, and we often visited with her and admired the beauty of the property. After Mr. Spiekerman's death, Mrs. Spiekerman, who had many relatives in the West, decided to sell the property, and my office took special interest, hunting for a buyer who would appreciate the unusual merits of the place. Finally, such a buyer appeared on the scene in the person of George W. Fennell, and after some negotiation we succeeded in bringing about a sale of the property to him in co-operation with Mr. George S. Meany who was at that time associated with my office. The property is on one of the highest spots in Greenwich and is often pointed out to visitors.

The sale of the estate of the late David M. Goodrich stands out very strongly in my memory. During his life, he had been a great friend of mine and had been associated with me actively as one of the enthusiastic followers of Theodore Roosevelt. David Goodrich's property was situated on the Mount Kisco-Millwood Road and was an ideal gentleman's farm. After his death, the property was placed on the market, and Mr. Hyatt showed it to a developer, Mr. I. W. Panzer, who had been very active in real-estate promotions. Mr. Panzer recognized the merits of the property and decided to purchase it for development if attractive terms could be arranged. I personally conducted the negotiations with the Bank of New York and Fifth Avenue Bank, who represented the estate. We finally brought about a sale, and Mr. Panzer proceeded to develop the property, which today is recognized generally as one of the most desirable residential districts in the Chappaqua area.

At this time, a very interesting sale was made by Mr. Terrell Van Ingen, in co-operation with Edward M. West, Inc., of property that we had much interest in, having sold it on two previous occasions. It was situated near Round Hill Road on a hilltop consisting of approximately eight acres of land where a house of rare charm had been built which was considered one of the finest estates in Greenwich. It belonged to Leonard Dalsemer, and Mr. Van Ingen brought about a sale to Mr. and Mrs. James Fetherolf.

I might also mention a sale which was made by my office at this time to the nephew of Mr. Henry J. Gaisman, who was one of my close friends. The nephew, Jacques C. Coleman, had become a good friend of our Mr. Hyatt and for quite a while had been searching for a home embodying every feature of farm life at its best and every comfort of a city house at its best. Such a property came into our hands for sale in the property of Jean Marcus. It was situated on the Seven Bridges Road, Chappaqua, and contained about seventy-three acres of land with a lovely colonial home, outbuildings, a private lake, an active stream, fields and woodland. I mention this as an interesting event in our many pleasant dealings with Mr. Gaisman and his family.

Previously we have referred to having purchased some of the land in the business section of Chappaqua and having had a great deal of activity in promoting the business district. Horace Greeley, one of the great men of his time, lived in Chappaqua, and his statue is prominently displayed at the Chappaqua Station. He built one of the first concrete houses constructed in the United States, overlooking the village. After his death, it was occupied by his family and finally his grandson, Mr. Frank Greeley Stahl, with whom we had very pleasant relations, put the property on the market. Mr. Bain Turner who was associated with us was in close contact with Mr. Henry B. Zeiger, president of the Ready Homes Corporation. After some negotiation, he purchased it for subdivision and development. This sale attracted considerable attention and I must say that we were honored in being the brokers.

Also during this period, our New York office sold for Mrs. Strook her country house near Ossining to Mr. Hirsch. Also, we sold the estate of Mr. E. A. Thomson, which was one of the finest farm estates near Carmel in Putnam County, to Mr. Elliot Simpson, one of New York City's successful business leaders. This was without question one of the best planned farm estates near New York. In addition to a well-planned main residence, it included a farmer's house and farm buildings where blooded cattle and superior farm products could be raised. Mr. Simpson and his wife were both people of good taste, and proceeded to add to, improve and decorate the residence.

The Elliot Simpson Estate in Carmel.

One sale which I will always remember, was the sale in 1945, of a Swiss chalet belonging to Casper J. Voorhis in the Long Ridge district of Stamford, Connecticut. Here was a house which in its exterior appearance looked like a large but well-proportioned log cabin. It was on a wooded ridge overlooking a private lake surrounded by dense woods. The interior of the house had excellent up-to-date appointments and featured a large living room opening out on a large covered porch commanding lovely views of the private lake, which had been created by damming the Mill River. In every way, the house gave one the feeling of being in one of the enchanting mountain areas of Switzerland. Mr. Ernest C. Geier and his wife, who had lived near White Plains in Westchester, fell in love with the place at first sight, and I sold it to them. They moved in and so arranged it that one had a deep feeling of complete country restfulness and natural beauty. I could easily understand why Mrs. Geier viewed it as paradise.

But now I have one of the saddest events in my experience to relate. One day Mrs. Geier and her brother who was visiting them went out for a row in their boat on the lake, when suddenly the canoe turned over and both were drowned. The neighbors, who had the highest regard for Mrs. Geier, were shocked and grieved beyond words.

Benenson Estate in Stamford.   Estate of Otto Marks in Stamford.

CHAPTER XIX

RECENT TRENDS

IN THE EARLY MONTHS of 1946, we made a sale in Riverdale-on-the-Hudson, in the northern part of New York City, which deserves comment. As I have said, the parkway along Riverside Drive, known as the Hudson River Parkway, was extended northward up to Spuyten Duyvil, and then a bridge was constructed in 1936 crossing Spuyten Duyvil Creek, leading the parkway through Riverdale and then through Yonkers and continuing north into what is now known as Taconic Parkway. With the building of this parkway, the picture of Riverdale and Spuyten Duyvil began to change rapidly. It had been considered a secluded country-like area, inaccessible to general transportation. With the building of the parkway and bridge across Spuyten Duyvil, this whole area became just uptown New York, making possible fast automobile transportation to downtown New York. Immediately the land of the Johnson estate began to be subdivided, and tall apartment houses sprang up on all sides. Zoning laws were liberal. The large Douglass estate was subdivided, and the large estates in Riverdale of families who had lived there for many years began to change, as intensive development crowded nearer and nearer. One of these estates which had been built by the New York builder Anthony Campagna, for his own use, consisted of a very large stone mansion on a magnificent site overlooking the Hudson River. As their family grew up and married, Mr. and Mrs. Campagna decided to sell and get a smaller house, and the property was listed with us for sale. The demand for large country houses in this district had declined, and we realized that it was going to be difficult to find a suitable buyer for the Campagna estate. But a bright light appeared. Important corporations which had their central offices in the heart of New York City began to consider moving to the suburbs. In many cases, this made it more accessible and pleasant for their employees and executives, and in many ways it was advantageous for the companies. One such company was the Monitor Equipment Company. We learned that they wished to move to a suburban location like Riverdale, and approached them. After learning their requirements, it occurred to us to show them the Campagna estate on Independence Avenue in Riverdale. After careful consideration, they agreed with us that it would, with minor alterations, serve their purposes excellently. Furthermore, their executive offices would help the neighborhood and not harm its residential appearance. We were successful in making a sale of the property to them.

About this same time, other large corporations, including several insurance companies, adopted this policy and many have moved into the suburban districts of Westchester County.

I might stop here for a minute to report that the beautiful Rickard property in New Canaan which we had sold to the popular authoress, Mignon Eberhart, was resold by our office to Lionel J. Noah, Jr., whose father had been a very good friend of mine.

Our office at this time had been very active in the hills of Stamford, and I had often admired a country estate that had been developed by Mr. Maitland Smith on Haviland Road in the Hunting Ridge district. A long and artistic private entrance road starting at Haviland Road and running along a picturesque brook and pond lead to the main house which was of modest size with many luxurious features. Next to it was a guest house of modest size, and both residences looked out over a large and beautiful private lake on the property, on one side of which was a swimming pool and covered pavilion. Near the main house, was a large garage with excellent servants' quarters and on the grounds nearby were farm buildings, including farmer's cottage, stable and a playhouse with guest quarters. In fact, the entire property was the type that the present day wealthy family in the city visions as an ideal country home. Mr. Smith listed the property for sale. Among our many clients was a New York business leader, Mr. Harold Cooper, who had also been active in the purchase and sale of New York real estate. After extensive search, he and his wife agreed with me that the Smith property came nearest to their requirements and decided to buy it. It was attractive when they bought it, but Mrs. Cooper with exquisite taste proceeded to improve it until today it stands out as a model of the highest type.

Some years previously, we had sold an estate on a hilltop near Mount Kisco in Westchester County, New York, to Mr. Samuel Kappel who several years later listed the property with us for sale. Mr. Ralph Straus, one of the younger members of the Straus family which developed the Macy Stores, had come to us to inquire about country houses. His requirements were difficult, but finally he settled on the estate of Mr. Kappel situated on a site not far from Mount

Kisco with large acreage including fields, woodland, farm buildings and horse stables, and above all else a large swimming pool. After some negotiation, we sold the property to Mr. Straus. The property was certainly in a most desirable neighborhood which had attracted many other substantial families to locate there, including Miss Anne Morgan, the daughter of J. P. Morgan, and R. S. Brewster of Brewster Body fame.

About this time, our office sold another property in Mount Kisco which attracted much interest. Colonel William Schiff had a large house on a fine hilltop location which had always been considered one of the most attractive estates in this area. We were fortunate in having among our clients Dr. Grant Sanger. His mother, Mrs. Margaret Sanger, had for years been a leader on the subject of birth control. Her many activities had given her great prominence. After careful study of all available properties, Dr. Sanger decided to buy the Schiff estate which we had strongly recommended, and our office was happy and highly honored in having made the sale.

One of the sales which I personally made at this time was that of the Sumner estate in Round Hill, Greenwich. Mr. Sumner, who was one of New York's leading lawyers, had been my very good friend. We often rode into New York from Greenwich together on the commuting train, and he would tell me of the pleasure which he had

The estate of Ralph Straus in Mount Kisco.

enjoyed in building up his country estate, which included a large acreage with a very private lake, extensive woodland, beautiful fields, a stone residence of English design and farm buildings. It was indeed one of the most ideal country estates that I had ever seen. After his death, the property was placed on the market, and I began to make a search for the type of buyer who would be interested. One of our clients was the late Baron Charles Neuman de Vegvar who had come to this country from Europe with a real understanding and appreciation of fine country estates. When he and his very brilliant and attractive wife inspected the property, I saw at once that it appealed to them very much. The Baroness even began to discuss where she could hang her rare paintings and place her art objects and furniture. They did not need all of the land, but would want a good part of it, including the lake. I succeeded in having the estate sell to the Baron that part of it which he was interested in purchasing, and I must add that he and the Baroness improved and maintained it beautifully. The balance of the estate was later sold and divided into various large sites on which fine suburban homes have been built.

In the period preceding World War II, Mrs. William Blake who had lived in upper Westchester County near Cross River, decided to purchase a large tract of land on the Stanwich Road in the northwest corner of the Stamford Hills on the boundary line of Greenwich. It overlooked the famous Mianus Gorge with its magnificent scenery. From its high ridge it commanded views way out to Long Island Sound. On this site, Mrs. Blake, who had traveled in Europe often, decided to build a house similar to many of the fine estates which she had admired there. It included every modern convenience and also featured many of the luxurious attractions of the great estates abroad, among them being very high ceilings, a very large living room and reception room, a beautifully panelled large dining room and library, numerous bedrooms and baths. In fact, the house had every feature necessary for gracious and luxurious living. After Mrs. Blake's death, the property was sold by the estate and finally purchased by Mr. A. Unger, head of Ansonia De Luxe Shops. Several years later he placed the property on the market. We showed the property to some of our clients but it was too big.

One day a young couple, Mr. and Mrs. Frank Hosford, inquired about houses for sale, and I escorted them around. None seemed large enough, so I finally decided to show them the Blake estate. To my surprise, they decided it was what they wanted, and I made a

artistic residence in North Greenwich remodeled by Ina Claire.

Main residence on the Sumner Estate purchased by the late Baron Neuman de Vegvar.

sale. They moved in and as time went on children were born and the family increased, and now the house was not too big. After some years, the Hosfords decided to move to the West, and the house was sold to a developer, Harry Schacter, one of the ablest leaders in the business. He sold it to a buyer who made it into the luxurious Deercrest Golf Club. Such are the changes and the unpredictable results which often have followed the building of country estates.

CHAPTER XX

MOVING FURTHER IN THE SUBURBS

DURING THE PERIOD after World War II, many projects and improvements which had been planned before the war and put in abeyance during the war were revived and great building activity both public and private got under way. Roads and parkways blossomed on all sides. Commercial and industrial structures, apartment houses and private homes arose on all sides. This did not take effect in Westchester County as much as in other areas because zoning and building restrictions protected the towns and villages from unwise and often very unattractive and undesirable development. Nevertheless, considerable improvement and building of the better type was undertaken. The sections in which our office was most active kept us very busy, and we found ourselves widening and extending our selling efforts way beyond the nearby suburbs. Many of our clients living in these nearby suburbs began to look further out to more rural districts.

One of the outstanding examples of this was the decision of the family of Mr. A. H. Sulzberger, editor of *The New York Times,* to move from their estate near White Plains to a more rural location. Mrs. Sulzberger's father, Adolph S. Ochs, the head of *The New York Times,* had purchased, remodelled and beautified an estate on North Street, White Plains, which was considered one of the finest specimens of colonial country house architecture in Westchester County. His daughter was Mrs. A. H. Sulzberger whose husband was the right hand of Mr. Adolph S. Ochs in publishing the paper. When Mr. Ochs died, Mr. and Mrs. Sulzberger occupied the Ochs mansion as their country house, but as time rolled by, they decided to sell the property and purchase another farther out in the country. Our office listed the property and made every effort to find a suitable purchaser, but had very little success because the mansion was too large for present day requirements. The main house included a large entrance hall, a very large and elaborate living room, a large sunroom, a library, office, a very large dining room, extensive kitchen facilities, a very large entertainment room on the basement level, many bedrooms and baths on the second floor, also many servants' rooms and baths, and on the third floor a large office arrangement where Mr. Ochs had done much of his editorial work. The grounds contained many acres of land including a private lake. The outbuildings included a superintendent's cottage, farm buildings, and garages. Near the main house was a swimming pool. All in all, the estate was a picture of luxurious country life.

Finally, in reply to one of our advertisements, Mr. Alexander Safie, a New York merchant who had spent a large part of his life in Colombia, South America, made inquiry. In Colombia there are large estates with fine houses, and Mr. Safie and his family decided that the Sulzberger estate was just what they wanted. After long negotiation, we arranged a sale of the property to Mr. Safie, but we were confronted with the problem of finding quickly a suitable country home for Mr. and Mrs. Sulzberger to move to. After considerable search, we finally had them inspect a very attractive colonial residence on a hilltop in the Long Ridge district of Stamford which had been built a short time previously by George W. Hill, Jr., the son of the late George W. Hill, the president of the American Tobacco Company, and was now for sale. It was excellently designed and included many arrangements which provided space for Mr. and Mrs. Sulzberger to place some of their furniture. It did not take long for the Sulzbergers to make up their minds, and they purchased the estate which is indeed a most delightful one, situated on a hilltop overlooking a private lake in a most desirable location, to which they have added much distinction.

Many other sales greatly interested me. One of them was the sale of the large estate of Senator David A. Reed on Dan's Highway in northern New Canaan which Mr. Terrell Van Ingen brought about, to Mrs. Hugette Clarke, the daughter of the late Senator Clarke. The drives, trees, active brook and gardens which one saw in driving up to the main house were entrancing. Mrs. Clarke, who had an apartment on Fifth Avenue in New York, decided to acquire a country home of merit. Senator Reed of Pennsylvania, who had for many years been developing his most artistic home in New Canaan, had decided to sell, and we were most fortunate in having it listed. When we learned of Mrs. Clarke's desire to purchase a country home, we felt that Senator Reed's home was almost made to order for her requirements. We made an appointment to have her visit the property, and it appealed to her. We succeeded in bringing about a sale. Senator Reed, who had deep sentimental interest in the estate, was very much pleased that it would become the property of a very distinguished new owner.

Our office was also very proud of the sale of the late Robert T. Swaine's estate, situated on Spring Valley Road on the easterly borderline of the Town of Lewisboro in Westchester County, New York, to Mrs. Herbert Straus whose late husband had been a member of the Straus family already mentioned. Mrs. Straus had sold her country estate in New Jersey and wished to acquire another in the hill country of Westchester or nearby Connecticut. Her home in New Jersey had been outstanding in every way, and it was very difficult to find one that would satisfy her requirements. However, we finally found one. It had been the result of the great imagination and great effort of Mr. and Mrs. Swaine. Here was a colonial house of superb architecture situated well back from the road in a lovely country area, on a large tract of land with excellent outbuildings. It was ample enough for gracious living, but not too large. After Mr. Swaine's death, Mrs. Swaine decided to sell the property. When I inspected it, I was spellbound. It was one of the most attractive that I had ever seen. When we were selecting properties to submit to Mrs. Straus, we found that the Swaine estate was by far the most attractive. After careful consideration, Mrs. Straus advised us that she would consider the purchase of the estate if a satisfactory price could be agreed upon. We consulted with Mrs. Swaine and the sale was made. It is indeed one of the finest and best-planned country homes in that area.

The estate of Mrs. Herbert Straus in Lewisboro, Westchester County, New York, near New Canaan, Connecticut.

An interesting sale made by our office at this time was a property owned by Lawrence Park Properties, Inc., situated on Midland Avenue near Bronxville. The property consisted of about thirteen acres of land, and the zoning regulations permitted the construction of apartment houses. It was near the famous Cross County Shopping Center which had recently been completed, and because of its location and environment would attract desirable tenants if apartments of quality were constructed. Nuovo Brothers, Inc. were one of our clients searching for such a property, and after some negotiation, Mr. L. P. Russell made a sale to them, and they proceeded to construct what we believe is one of the most attractive garden apartment developments in the New York suburbs.

In the period following World War II, many fine acreage tracts in Westchester which had been purchased for the building of gentlemen's farm estates were again placed on the market. Such a property was that of Richard Croker, Jr., the son of Richard Croker, former leader of Tammany Hall in New York who owned a tract of land in the town of Rye extending from Ridge Road to King Street. It was a beautiful site on a high elevation with lovely fields, commanding views of the surrounding country. This property was purchased by Mr. and Mrs. Robert Law. They wanted to build an ideal country

e very attractive apartments built by Nuovo Bros. near Bronxville.

The final development of the Valentine Terrace property situated on Valentine Lane and Riverdale Avenue, Yonkers.

house and employed Dwight J. Baum, the architect who had earned a high reputation in the Fieldston-Riverdale district. Mr. Baum designed a house of English architecture which won great praise. It was pictured in the architects' magazine as one of the finest houses of the year. The Laws developed the land and actually built a small private golf course on the grounds. It was indeed a show place, and they enjoyed it for many years. Finally they decided to sell, and the property was acquired by George Baldwin who offered it for sale.

At the time I had a client, Mr. Samuel Katz, who had a country estate in New Jersey where he had raised a very fine herd of pure bred Guernsey cows. This was a hobby which he enjoyed very much. He and his wife decided that they would like to have a country home in Westchester where they could keep their champion cattle. I showed them all the properties which I thought would meet their requirements, but none interested them until they visited the Law estate. After Mr. Katz acquired the property he proceeded to make many extensive improvements. He purchased adjoining property and built the latest and best of modern stables. It was not only one of the finest country homes, but became a leading Guernsey farm in this section of the country. I often visited the estate and words fail me to describe its many charms. One day Mr. Katz told me that he had had the misfortune of being stricken with heart trouble, and his doctor had told him that he must take it easy and discontinue the strenuous activities which he had undertaken in breeding cattle. He had finally decided to sell his herd, and he and Mrs. Katz wanted to sell the estate and acquire a smaller one, preferably on the water front of Long Island Sound. I showed the estate to buyers, and on one occasion had come very close to making a sale. Finally, the thought occurred to me to offer it to Mr. Irving Chanin, the New York builder who had a home in Premium Point, New Rochelle, and who had purchased and modernized the beautiful Agar estate near his home which had come on the market after the death of Mr. Agar. Mr. Chanin was offering it for sale, and knowing that he was a most able real-estate developer, I suggested that perhaps I could get Mr. Katz to take the Agar property in part payment if Mr. Chanin purchased the Katz estate which would make a wonderful real-estate development. When Mr. Chanin visited the Katz property, he readily saw the wonderful opportunity it offered. When Mr. and Mrs. Katz visited the Agar estate, they concluded that it would serve their requirements. The result was a long negotiation and a final agreement to sell. Titles to

The magnificent Samuel Katz Estate in Rye.

the properties were exchanged. Two days later we were all deeply shocked and grieved in learning that Mr. Katz had had a severe heart attack which caused his death.

Mr. Chanin had already made plans for the development of the Katz estate, but, in the meantime, other developments which he had undertaken were taking up very much of his time, and the Katz development was delayed. Others who were in the market for land for development began to make inquiries about its possible resale by Mr. Chanin. Finally he sold it to the Country Ridge Estates, who are now developing the property into a beautiful residential park with many homes. Whenever I pass the property I am very proud of having had even a small part in its history.

CHAPTER XXI

INTERESTING RECENT SALES

ON JANUARY 1, 1954, our office decided to move from the City of New York and conduct its entire operations in Westchester County and nearby Connecticut, because the traffic congestion had become so great that it was difficult for people to come in from the country to see us in the city to discuss their real estate problems. We finally settled on locating our main Westchester office in the village of Chappaqua, where we had had much activity in the past. We also, for a while, had an office at 62 West Putnam Avenue in Greenwich, but finally consolidated our entire efforts in the Chappaqua office.

The development of the middle and upper section of Westchester County and nearby Connecticut has indeed been very intensive. Fortunately, excellent zoning laws have been adopted in various communities for the prevention of congestion and deterioration of neighborhoods as has often happened in other suburbs, with the result that Westchester County is a most beautiful and likeable country area appealing to the best taste and most exacting requirements of many of our citizenship. It will continue in the highest sense to be the home place which they deeply love.

Shortly after we had located our main office in Chappaqua, Mr. J. Bain Turner, one of our associates, succeeded in interesting one of our clients, Dr. John J. Dolce, in investing in the business area of Chappaqua. A beautiful new store building had recently been built on Greeley Avenue and was excellently tenanted. Dr. Dolce recognized the merits of the property and purchased it. He also purchased an attractive corner building, the first floor of which had been the town office and the second floor the headquarters of the New York Telephone Company, and another parcel of vacant land on North Greeley Avenue nearby. These sales were a good indication of how the development of business property in Chappaqua was and will continue to be an excellent investment. The amount of land zoned for business use is limited, and the neighborhood is of a quality appealing to the best type of stores.

Mr. Turner also made a sale at about this time which made us very proud. Mr. I. J. Fox, the head of the fur establishment, had

The outstanding country estate of the late I. J. Fox near Harmon, Westchester County.

developed a beautiful estate near Harmon in upper Westchester County, containing approximately 100 acres of land, a private lake which he had created by building a large dam, and had constructed a house of the most up-to-date type with every advantage. There was also a large swimming pool with a cabaña, dining terrace, a guest house of exceptional charm, farm buildings; in fact, everything that the most exacting seekers of a country estate would ordinarily desire. After his death, the property was placed on the market and was shown by us to many clients, but was so far above the average requirement that it was hard to find a purchaser. Mr. Turner succeeded in interesting Dr. Murray B. Weiner in the property, and finally brought about the sale to him. A sale which we were very proud to make at this time was the M. B. Hertzig estate in Armonk which Mrs. Jacques A. Mitchell of our office sold to Mr. Robert W. Sarnoff, Chairman of the Board of the National Broadcasting Company. Mr. Sarnoff's father is David Sarnoff, president of the Radio Corporation of America, who was a close friend and associate of Mr. E. J. Nally, the first president of the Radio Corporation of America, with whom we had many very pleasant real estate transactions as previously mentioned in these reminiscences.

On North Street in Greenwich, an estate which had been developed by James R. McKee came on the market and was subdivided. The house was a brick Georgian colonial residence of splendid layout. However, it needed modernization and decoration, and had been purchased by Mrs. George Whitmore, my step-daughter, for renovation and resale. She succeeded in selling it to Mr. Horace Vernet, who made it his residence. Changes in Mr. Vernet's plans brought about a decision to sell this very lovely estate, and I happened to have a client, Mr. Ralph B. Wyman, who was residing in Greenwich but wanted a much larger house. After the most careful consideration, Mr. Wyman and his wife decided to purchase the property, and I succeeded by long-distance telephone to bring about a sale from Mr. Vernet who was then in Florida. As one passes the house on North Street with its high stone wall, one realizes the expense which many of our estate builders incurred in creating their lovely homes. Homes which could not be duplicated today.

In 1954, one of my good friends and clients, Mr. Otto Marks, a Wall Street broker, who had purchased a beautiful water front estate in Orienta Point, Mamaroneck, decided to move from that area, which was rapidly being subdivided and developed, to a more country-like district. We discussed the matter at length. I showed him many properties and finally took him to see an estate on the Westover Road, Stamford, which had been put on the market by the owner, Mrs. Ruby Schinasi. She had purchased the property some years before, and improved it in such a fashion that it would appeal to the most exacting buyer. The property contained many acres of land. It was approached by a long beautiful avenue of trees. It overlooked the Mianus River which had been dammed up at this point, creating a private lake suitable for all water sports, swimming, fishing and boating. A bridge across this lake leads to a beautiful forest with paths for walking. Overlooking the lake was a well-planned beach house with cooking and dining facilities. In every way it was appealing. Mr. Marks and his wife decided that the Schinasi house more nearly met their requirements than any property that they had inspected. We sold it to them. They have enjoyed the property so thoroughly, that I have been very happy in being the broker who brought about the sale.

Several years ago, Mrs. Walter Pforzheimer, whose husband had recently died, had a conversation with me relative to the sale of her house and a large tract of land which her husband had accumulated during his lifetime. The property was situated on Purchase Street in Purchase in lower Westchester, and was without question one of the most desirable tracts of land which could be used for development. She authorized me to offer the property for sale, and I proceeded to do so, offering it to several of my investing clients to whom I believed it would make a strong appeal. After very extensive study, Mr. Mac Gache, a most successful real-estate investor, authorized me to make an offer to purchase the property, which he planned to develop in a manner which would appeal to exacting home seekers. Mrs. Pforzheimer, who was not living in the house, but had moved to an apartment in New York, finally agreed to accept the terms of Mr. Gache, and I am sure that this will prove to be one of the most successful development undertakings in the nearby Westchester suburbs.

Another attractive sale at this time was made by me to some friends, Mr. and Mrs. George S. Hunt. Mr. and Mrs. Hunt had rented a home in Greenwich for the summer, and also maintained an apartment in New York. They finally decided that they would like to make Greenwich their year-round home, and I made a most careful study of all the properties which I thought would suit them. They finally selected the estate of Mr. M. T. Stark which had been developed on the Stanwich Road of Greenwich, overlooking a private lake, containing a colonial residence of moderate size, two additional cottages, a studio cottage and horse barns. Mr. Hunt was fond of riding, and this was indeed an ideal place for a horseman. Mr. Stark, the owner, had been a famous breeder of champion horses and won many a prize at the various horse shows. We succeeded in bringing about a sale of the estate to Mr. and Mrs. Hunt, and it certainly has become a residence of great happiness.

I have not mentioned in these reminiscences two sales which I have always been extremely happy to have taken an active part in. One was locating for my very attractive niece, Mrs. Everett Noetzel, and her husband a beautiful country home in Scarsdale, which is one of the show places of the district. She has taken a very active part in the public affairs of this area. Her husband, a vice president of the Borden Company, has been president of the Scarsdale Country Club. The couple are among the most popular of Scarsdale.

Another instance which I may include, is the sale to my very attractive daughter, Mrs. Lathrop Douglass, and her husband of part of the land in Greenwich which had been the estate of Percy Rockefeller. The site where Mr. Rockefeller's house had been situated was exceptionally interesting. The original house had been torn down some years ago, and my son-in-law, Lathrop Douglass, purchased its beautiful site. Mr. Douglass, a noted architect, designed a house of colonial architecture which is indeed a lovely home in every way.

This about winds up the narrative of some of the sales which my office has negotiated in the development of Westchester County and nearby Connecticut. We have made many other sales, some of which would undoubtedly prove equally interesting. The ones which I have included here are typical of the very pleasant and extensive events which it has been my good fortune to be a part of, and which I love to recall.

Douglass Residence in Greenwich.

Noetzel Residence in Scarsdale.

Dupont residence in Greenwich.

Wise Estate in Stamford.